EVERYTHING NEW IS FREE

Thoughts of
A Globetrotting Hotelier

PETER ALATSAS

Design by Feng Lei / AsiaMedia

Editing by Tina Kanagaratnam / AsiaMedia

ISBN-13: 978-0-9789658-0-8
ISBN-10: 0-9789658-0-9
Copyright © 2006 by Peter Alatsas

First edition 2006

Editor: Tina Kanagaratnam
Designer: Feng Lei

AsiaMedia

For Jahan & Arya

CONTENTS

EVERYTHING NEW IS FREE
Thoughts of a Globetrotting Hotelier

THE BUSINESS OF LIFE

FOOD FOR THOUGHT

POSTSCRIPT

PERSPECTIVES ON THE BUSINESS OF TRAVEL & LIFE

The most defining quality of a formidable intellect is the ability to accept life for what it is and the world for what it can become. The perspectives on life in this book about life are not new. The pursuit of happiness, the search for meaning and purpose is fundamental to all philosophical thinking. They have preoccupied humankind for centuries, and will undoubtedly continue to do so for many years to come.

Much of life is what we make of it. There are those who choose to think of their lives as a problem or a riddle to be solved rather than a precious gift to enjoy. Still others look backwards, recalling failures and lamenting missed opportunities and unfulfilled dreams. (If indeed "life is short", one wonders why it is wasted living in the past this way?)

We all want to make the best of our lives, to lead the lives we want. It all comes down to attitude, choices and destiny.

✦ **ATTITUDE IS EVERYTHING** Oscar Wilde once said: one's only life is the life one *never leads*. True for many, but does it have to be this way? Not with the right attitude. Attitude, of course, is as much a habit as anything else, and getting in a positive frame of mind has been well documented as being a powerful asset in dealing with all life's challenges.

The combination of *critical thinking* and the *right attitude*, for example, is a powerful combination — thinking and acting in terms of what is *appropriate* regardless of the circumstances rather than the more subjective notion of what is *right or wrong*.

Simple ideas, originating in real-life experience – but oftentimes the most difficult to apply because of the multiple perspectives, perceptions and combinations of differing attitudes. Persistence pays: everything is difficult before it becomes easy.

❖ **CHOICES** Our motivation and the choices we make determine the life we make for ourselves.

We live in a world that is driven and dominated by new technologies introduced at a furious pace. Keeping up is the new challenge. Keeping it all in proper perspective is another. We may be living in a predominantly technologically advanced and interconnected world yet we are, in the main, emotionally disconnected. The same technology that keeps us connected 24-7 "for convenience" disconnects us from quality time with family and friends. And paradoxically, the very technology that is supposed to make life easier and more convenient has taken away free time, making it difficult to live life to the fullest. Socializing and cultivating caring and meaningful personal relationships with others, so essential to happiness, harmony and a peaceful coexistence, is taking a back seat to this "busyness". *The less of routine, the more of life*, said A.B. Alcott. The choices, as always, are ours to make.

❖ **DESTINY** The universal search for meaning is often disguised as a yearning for discovering ones roots – returning to one's destiny. Here in China, we see children of the

Chinese diaspora, born and raised outside China, returning to discover their roots and to reacquaint themselves with their cultural values and heritage. As I watch them, I am reminded of my own experiences with cultural assimilation and integration in a very different place and time.

I am an exotic cocktail, an amalgamation of different experiences and cultures. I was born in Greece, raised in Australia, educated in Canada and in cyberspace (an MBA from Sheffield Business School acquired by distance learning). For the better part of the last three decades, I have lived around the world: in the United States, Saudi Arabia, Brunei, Malaysia, Singapore, Thailand, Indonesia, Japan and China.

I have felt the effects from cultural shock, rapid change over short periods of time in unfamiliar places. Generally speaking, I addressed most of them with the *right attitude.*

Almost everything I encountered was new and free. Free for me to either accept or reject. For instance, I made every reasonable effort to adjust, if I could not change, relative to what was appropriate and necessary at the time or what best suited the environment I happened to be in, I was free to choose between tolerance and intolerance; I chose the former and made every possible sincere effort to understand, respect and tolerate the differences in each place.

My experiences were not uncommon. We were the children of brave immigrant parents, escaping a Europe that had been ravaged by the Second World War. These immigrants arrived in the millions in the new world, full of hopes and dreams.

I recognize the predicament some of these young Chinese returnees are in, because I was in the same one, once. Torn between two lovers, trying to reconcile my traditional Greek cultural values with those in the West, and later in the East. (After all, history has indeed a way of repeating itself. As Harry Truman once said, in reference to change, *"the only thing new in the world is the history you don't know."*)

Still, there is hope for these young returnees. When I look back at my experience from my perspective today, I see that it has proved to be less traumatic and more an inspirational journey of discovery than anything else — a form of rebirth for me. My bicultural background and opportunities to travel, coupled with my life's work, the management of luxury hotels in diverse cultural settings, has given me and my family a more balanced view and a broader perspective of the world. More specifically, it has increased my level of understanding, acceptance and tolerance of other people and their cultures.

In the process I have learned, that in business as in life, *the effective management of people transcends culture.*

I also learned, *freedom to choose, together with our actions is what ultimately defines us.*

The inspiration for the title comes from an elderly Greek peasant man who was sitting next to me on a boat in the Mediterranean en route to the 'Holy Mountain' in northern Greece.

"Every time I come here I feel new... I see something new, and it's free," he said.

About the Quotations

One of the most delightful ways of acquiring wisdom is through the quotations of thinkers and philosophers from the past. Benjamin Disraeli offers a fitting explanation: *the wisdom of the wise and the experience of the ages are perpetu-*

ated by quotations. While a slightly different view is offered by Isaac D'Israel, who claims: *the wise make proverbs and fools repeat them.*

Quotations have been used throughout the book to complement my impressions on the business of travel and life. Many come from philosophers of one kind or another, many from antiquity, as their thoughts are still relevant today.

Most of the quotations come from the "axial period" (800-200 BC), or age of philosophers. Also known as the age of individual consciousness (in contrast with the "pre-axial period," characterized by a tribal consciousness), this period saw the appearance of the great Eurasian religions, around 500 BC.

The axial people, as defined by the German philosopher Karl Jaspers, are the Chinese, Iranians, Greeks, Jews and Indians. To them, he claims, *this axial period was a second birth, so to speak, and through it they laid the foundations of man's spiritual being.* During the axial period human values, ways of thinking and perceptions of the universe took place concurrently in diverse cultural centers around the world. Their main concerns were how to build a good and just society where people could be taught to regulate themselves.

Two ancient civilizations, Greece from the west and China from the east, were simultaneously engaged in radical changes and transformational endeavors. In Greece, there was the development of sciences, philosophy, "know thyself", and democracy, which changed the course of western history. In China, Confucius was developing his ideas about the individual's ethical path and a collective harmonious society. Lao Tzu, the founder of Taoism was creating a new way to perceive life through the stars and Buddha pioneered a path towards enlightenment and nirvana.

Buddha, the Jewish prophets and Plato lived at the same time. There are parallels, for example, between Zhuang Zi and Pythagoras, Confucius and Plato and Socrates, Sun Tzu and Alexander the Great. Given the inevitable intercourse, for primarily economic and cultural reasons at the time, between the cradles of Eastern and Western civilizations, the Greek spirit must have connected with ancient Chinese wisdom.

THE BUSINESS
OF TRAVEL

"To travel hopefully is better than to arrive."

—SIR JAMES JEANS

"Wheresoever you go, go with all your heart."

—CONFUCIUS

"Travel is the antidote to ignorance."

—PETER ALATSAS

The moon is rounder in foreign lands

—CHINESE SAYING

A ROUNDER MOON

Studying the classics in Greece as a teenager was indeed a happy time. Yet I had to leave beloved places and friends to realize my dream of becoming a world-class architect. I left, in search of my dreams and the rounder moon that the Chinese saying tells us we will find in foreign lands. And I became, not a world-class architect, but a world-class (traveling) hotelier.

The moon, as we know, is the same everywhere. What might make it different are our notions, perceptions, ambitions and dreams. There are, I suppose, just as many moons as there are people and just as many dreams. Traveling, in its simplest manifestation is an opportunity for discovery. A test of one's powers of imagination and inspiration, if you like. As I continue to put these to the test, I keep on searching for a rounder moon.

Whilst visiting in Melbourne recently, I was told the true story of the plight of a 16-year old Greek girl who came to Australia unescorted in the early 1950s as a "mail order" bride in search of a new life. (Mail order brides were a common practice in the Americas and Australia after both world wars.)

She was one of 300 or so mail order brides coming from various parts of ravaged Europe to start a new life in the new world, with its rounder moon. Finally, after many months at sea in rather squalid conditions, the ship docks at Victoria's Port Melbourne. Her first task is to locate her new husband, with only a photograph to go on. As the huge ship sails closer to the shore, she clutches the picture in one hand, and her meager belongings in the other, waiting anxiously to dock.

As soon as the ship docks, the pier ignites with humanity and hundreds of would-be couples, photographs in hand, scramble for hours to find one another. The young girl wanders through the crowd, in vain. But after closer inspection of the photograph in her hand, and of a well-dressed, middle-aged mustached man holding a simple bouquet of flowers (who she has passed several times), the bride realizes that she is holding a dated photograph of her now aging husband.

Her romantic dreams now dashed, penniless and demoralized, she is nonetheless unwilling to accept this older version of the younger man in her photograph. She decides to return home on the same ship. She pleads with the Captain, convincing him to take her back, so that she can return another day with new hope. Months later, she returns on the ship, presumably more experienced and much wiser than before. And this time, she succeeds, discovering the man of her dreams — the one that matches her new picture.

Discovery, after all, is not the sole domain of scientists and brainy people. Discovery, said Albert Szent Gyorgi, consists of "seeing what everyone else has seen and thinking what no one else has thought", whether it's a new husband or a new perspective. Enlightening thoughts for travelers and moon-gazers alike.

A pleasant and happy life does not come from external things. Man draws from within himself, as from a spring, pleasure and joy.

—Plutarch

WHIRLING IN ISTANBUL

People ask me, which is the most exotic city you have visited? Although well intended, this is a rather unfair and difficult question. There are so many exotic places. Add to that the fact that exotic, by definition, can be a rather vague term, especially in a diverse world of colorful cultures and traditions such as ours.

My own simple definition of exotic is a place or something that is totally unfamiliar. Based on this, I pick Bangkok and Istanbul. After all, can it get any more exotic than a Whirling Dervish?

I once met a real Dervish, who went by the nickname "Bohlool". I was absolutely fascinated with the old man and with his lifestyle. A frail gentleman, he was naturally congenial, with penetrating eyes that smiled at you, despite their age. I enjoyed locking eyes with him, and exchanging pleasantries with body language, since we did not share a common language. He had a distinctive, long white beard, which he would proudly twist at the bottom with his thumb and index finger each time we ran into each other on the street. This was a trademark habit of his (or some kind of neurotic tick). His sequenced cap and rugged colorful clothes gave the impression that he was a well-dressed poor man. He was indeed very poor, and depended on handouts, much like the Buddhist monks in saffron colored robes in Bangkok. Nevertheless, he lived the life of a spiritually rich and contented man, or so I was told by his many fans in the neighborhood. "He is as welcome as a sunny day", one of the street merchants told me in broken English. "No day is complete without seeing him." I came across a picture I had taken with him recently, rekindling memories and emotions. He is in another world now, spreading love.

Sufism is what "Bohlool" was all about. Sufism is an ancient mystical sect of Islam that emphasizes a personal religious experience of God as divine love. This is a moderate outward looking brand of Islam that is generally considered more tolerant. Jalal al Din Rumi, the 13th century Sufi Mystic and poet who lived in Turkey, was its founder. The whirling dance was a form of prayer and meditation for Sufis, although today, it is more a cultural rather than a religious expression. The practice stresses modern life and Islamic spirituality and is popular especially in religiously tolerant Turkey. Places of worship of all faiths, open to all visitors of all faiths, abound in Istanbul, an eternal world city, a city of exotic experiences, real and imagined.

(And Bangkok, you ask? That's for another time.)

One by One

Like beauty, one by one,
The beauty contestants come and go

The nadir of Nardini's emotions
In moist eyes seen and felt as,
One by one, the beauties left

Perhaps to change the world - theirs,
His, and our own

Emotions dormant memories
Until revived and renewed
Perhaps a year from now

Like the years, when new beauties,
One by one, will come and go

—PETER ALATSAS

The poem was inspired by the emotional farewell
to the Miss World contestants by Claudio Nardini,
general manager of the Sheraton Sanya Resort

LESSONS ON BEAUTY

Hotels, by their very natures, are social places, and the ones that become an intrinsic part of their communities are the ones that flourish. You know the ones I mean: the hotels – especially in Asia — that are magnets for the community's activities, where the lobbies are a walking "who's who". You never know whom you will bump into or what you might encounter, and this is part of their attraction and the fascination.

I stayed at one of these hotels recently, a luxury resort on beautiful Sanya beach, on the Chinese tropical island of Hainan. The attraction and the fascination during my visit was with the 100 beauty queens who were staying at the hotel while they competed in the Miss World pageant.

The competition, which took place over the course of several weeks, involved assessments of the contestants' capabilities and character in addition to looks. The physical beauty of the resort complemented the proceedings. Set against pristine Yalong Bay, the resort made a picture-perfect backdrop for the event, and the guests found themselves basking in the sun and in the sheer beauty of the moment as well. You can imagine the scene at beachside.

Those of us on-site could watch this unfold before us, but for the wider world, there was the televised pageant. I learned that most of the work and the decision-making actually takes place behind the scenes, in confidence, well in advance of the main event on television. Remarkably, many of the contestants had a hunch about their chances of winning. Several actually guessed the outcomes with remarkable accuracy, including predictions as to who would be the eventual winner. Somehow, deep inside, we all know our net worth when it comes to physical attributes.

I was surprised to learn that each of the contestants had a 'licensee'. These are entrepreneurs who purchase the rights to represent beauty queens, both winners and losers, for a year. These entrepreneurs then charge for the privilege of inviting a beauty queen or a celebrity, for photo taking and mingling with guests, thus adding sparkle to the event. Celebrities have a way of helping to illuminate events with their presence, and they needn't utter so much as a word. What price beauty? These entrepreneurs know.

Don't worry about being misunderstood but about understanding others

—CONFUCIUS

MYSTICAL BALI

As recently as the early 1990s, Bali was relatively un-known as a vacation spot to mainstream tour agents and mainstream travelers. It was more famous than popular. Famous because mainly movie stars and wealthy individuals could afford to find and enjoy such an exotic place. However, with the development of internationally branded four- and five-star resorts and enclaves such as Nusa Dua — a self contained luxury beachside community consisting mainly of resorts, shopping centers and golf courses — tourism picked up considerably in a relatively short period of time, making it the popular destination it is today.

Bali is predominantly Hindu. Some people still think of Bali as a separate country, unaware that it is part of Indonesia, the world's largest Muslim country. Though Bali's brand of Hinduism is different than India's, it is nevertheless mystical. These contrasts are also part of the appeal. The Balinese are polite and gentle to the point of meekness. They lead a collective existence, a style of communal living. They are superstitious, and much of their waking life is devoted to festivals and rituals.

I often walked the grounds of the resort I managed there at different times of the day, to make inspections and later, share my observations with the management team. As General Manager, it was the easiest task I had to perform. Vacationers had discovered a banana tree with bananas at one end of the resort, which then became a favorite photo spot. Every so often, I would notice the bananas missing even though I had given instructions that they were not to be cut down, since the tree was so popular. Finally, one of the Managers, after having mustered enough courage to end this cat-and-mouse game, leveled with me: the bananas were being cut down by staff so that evil spirits would not feed on them. Without bananas, the spirits would starve, or go somewhere else.

Faced with this dilemma, I decided to employ a technique we had been using with a coconut tree on the property. Each evening, a member of staff would climb this beachside tree and fill a net hidden just under the leaves with coconuts. The next morning, another member of staff (affectionately nicknamed "the monkey") climbed the tree to "pluck" coconuts for paying customers. This fun activity was a popular photo op and a novel way to get a drink of coconut juice at the same time. We were always honest with our guests, explaining the "trick" after the fact. Guests were amused, and to my knowledge, no one had ever asked for their money back.

So, why not do the same with the banana tree? Only this time, the bananas went up during the day and came down during the night. I must confess, however, that my regular after dark inspection routine which had previously included walking under this particular banana tree, became slightly modified, even after the bananas had been removed. Yes, I detoured away from the tree, and the possibility of evil spirits. Why take a chance? When in Bali, do as the Balinese do. The staff, needless to say, was delighted with my newfound attitude.

A good style must, first of all, be clear. It must.... be appropriate

—A<small>RISTOTLE</small>

LOOK UP:

THE TEACHINGS OF
BUDAPEST ARCHITECTURE

The day I arrived in Budapest, celebrations of the re-building of the Bridge of Mostar were in full swing on television. As I listened to the proceedings, I looked out from my hotel window and saw the majestic city skyline and the famous Danube. The bridge in question was built by the Ottoman Turks in the Islamic style and destroyed in 1993 during the Bosnian war. Some 260,000 died and 1.8 million people were displaced in the conflict. The rebuilding of a bridge symbolized hope for a new beginning – and I added my own wish: "let's hope the new bridge will also come to symbolize the senseless brutality of war."

I had yearned to visit Budapest and its legendary beauty for myself ever since I was a youngster. I wasn't disappointed. The city is an amalgamation of two cities, with the river Danube running in between - "Buda" on one side of its banks, and "Pest" on the other. Rich in history and culture as well as beauty, Budapest has also had its share of conflict and invaders. Here too, things are looking up: EU membership has been a key turning point.

The moment I hit the streets, though, my motivation turned from history to architecture. Budapest's old buildings are some of the finest I've seen anywhere – this, despite the fact that many are in disrepair and in great need of modernization and rejuvenation. The city is a magnet for entrepreneurs, architects and designers, with enough work to keep creatives busy for centuries.

The renovation of the old Grisham Palace and its subsequent conversion into the slick Four Seasons hotel is a case in point. The neoclassical style structure, with Art Deco interiors is a must-see (even if you cannot afford to stay there). Directly opposite the hotel is the famous chain bridge, its entrance flanked by two lions. According to legend, a young boy noticed that the lions were missing their tongues, and mentioned this to the architect. Embarrassed and humiliated, the architect committed suicide by jumping off the bridge. (Unlike at Mostar, this was, I suppose, far more appropriate than blowing up the bridge.)

As I continued on my architectural tour, I kept looking up, above the distractions — the glitz and glamor of neon lights and decals at street level. These obstacles of modernity often obscure beautiful architecture, not only in Budapest but in all cities around the world. Paradoxically, treasures of cultural and artistic value, in the open for all to see, become hidden. For in not looking up, we simply fail to see.

Liberty is being free from the things we don't like in order to be slaves to the things we do like

—ERNEST BENN

BROWSING IN BRUGGE

Brussels was nicer the first time around. Going back seemed somewhat anticlimactic. So I went to Brugge. From Brussels, the short train ride to this medieval city was a joy. It was like going back in time, to the middle ages. To a time when bell towers (such as the 80-meter high one in Brugge) were skyscrapers, so much so that they were used as watchtowers for fires. This small city is a living museum, much like Venice, Kyoto and Zhouzhuang, on the outskirts of Shanghai.

This serene place is a magnet for artists, as well. Horse-drawn carriages, the indelible sounds of horse's hooves on cobblestone streets, and remarkable architecture are everywhere. The vistas and the romance they invoke are inspirational. The impressive structures form a pretty mosaic of buildings of different architectural styles: ancient Roman and Greek, Gothic and Renaissance. The numerous canals that weave through this quaint village are most delightful. If time is of the essence, the best way to experience Brugge is by tourist boat. There are many available, with professional guides who will expertly navigate you through this beauty in the most time efficient way.

I was surprised to learn that the first stock exchange was established here, and of the significance of the city as a key shipping and trading center. Today, all that is past, and the lesson of history seems to be that the line between greatness and fallen greatness is a fine one. Great cities continue to flourish only with enlightened leadership – leadership that is able to foresee needed changes and then turn them into reality. All too often, changes are made only by action-forcing events. In such cases, it is often too late. Better to anticipate change than to react to it. (The same is generally true for people.)

Similarly, people today walk the line between living for today and planning for the future, yet these are not mutually exclusive. Both are essential for quality of life. At the heart of quality living is making free time to enjoy life. The same could be said about travel. Travel, to my mind, is more a necessity than a luxury. It is a means of nourishing mind and body, no less important to well-being than food and water.

An ounce of image is worth a pound of performance

—LAURENCE J. PETER

FORTRESS MANILA

Travel is a multi-faceted endeavor. Hotels, for one, play a key role in the process. Take the so-called "stay experience", which can make or break a trip. The tangible physical aspects have become commodities nowadays, so much so that most hotels compete almost entirely on the intangibles: that is, the emotional and spiritual aspects of a stay, in the form of service excellence. Hand to heart, they promise their customers (guests in hotel parlance), that all their needs will be met "whatever, whenever, and wherever" they want. It takes teams of altruists and dedicated people with pathos for pleasing people to deliver consistently on such brand promises.

Hotels are social places where sometimes the dreams and fantasies of end users materialize. People come to hotels sometimes because they need a bed for a night in a strange place, but just as often, they come to escape or to affirm who they are or who they aspire to be. And there's little doubt that their aura of glamour means that they hold a special fascination for many people.

Hotels function as guesthouses, centers for commerce and social activity, fun and enjoyment. Yet very real global security concerns have transformed some of them into fortress-like camps, resembling prisons in many respects. I still recall the extra security measures taken by hotels in Manila. The hotel I stayed at had guards posted at every door, with electronic metal scanner devices searching people and their belongings. Dogs were patrolling the lobby, sniffing for bombs relentlessly around the clock.

(One woman I noticed wearing a mini skirt was particularly concerned with trying to keep the dogs at bay.) How much protection is enough, I pondered? I truly empathized with the good people trying to run the hotel as a normal business, in addition to protecting us from harm.

Fixed electronic means of surveillance, as opposed to blatantly visible ones, are less threatening and help preserve the romantic allure, functionality, and that special bond people have with hotels. Surveillance cameras are becoming standard features in underground parking lots, elevators and public areas, and this is most welcome. However, hotel elevators programmed to access floors with electronic room keys are not an industry standard and this has to change. Every hotel should have this capability as a minimum for added safety, security and peace of mind for both operators and end users.

Search for the ultimate protection device as we might, there is no fool-proof security system. I hope the day never comes when hotels are forced to operate like prison camps. I hope we are never forced to give up a vital part of our society – and our dreams.

Study the past if you would divine the future

—CONFUCIUS

34

IRAN: LOST IN POLITICS

Almost three decades have passed since I heard echoes of gunshots ringing in the distance from the safety of a rooftop villa in Tehran's fashionable Tajrish district. It was the beginning of the Iranian revolution. Only I did not know it then. I remember being overcome by selfishness and confusion. In a matter of seconds my delightful mood had changed. It wasn't so much the shots in the dark that scared me, as I was due to leave in a few days, but the thought of saying goodbye to my magnanimous hosts and the caring people I had come to know. Perhaps I may never see them or this beautiful exotic place again, I thought. Profound changes have indeed taken place since that time and, as fate would have it, I have not returned.

Fond memories, however, have a way of enduring. What is noticed and what is remembered is not the same. While we notice objects and impressive physical surroundings, what stands out most is the kindness of people. Although the local authorities encourage tourism these days, there is reluctance to travel to Iran. The chance to experience this culturally rich land has been lost in politics. Part of the reason for this reluctance is the misconception that confuses Iran with the Middle East and the Arab World. Iranians are Persians, not Arabs. One could characterize them as Indo-Europeans, quite distinct from other nations in the region. Circumstances have compelled them to lead what many observers call a double life: one private, one public. A juggling act, from my personal observations, that only they can perform, with style and dignity.

I have a special affinity for this land both historically and personally. After all, Greek history and Persian history are intertwined. Much of ancient history comes to us from Greek historians who characterized the Persians as foes and barbarians. From a purely intellectual standpoint it is important to filter out any potentially inherent biases like this — let's not go there.

Let's go to Persepolis instead. This is where Alexander the Great defeated Darius the Great, thus ending the great Persian Empire, which had flourished for centuries. Alexander was so impressed with this city that he chose it as the place to integrate the Greek and Persian races through intermarriage. (It didn't work.) Esfahan is another fabled city, with its magnificent Imam Square. It was originally known as the *naqsh-e-jahan* square, which means the map of the world, because each corner is meant to represent the points of the compass. It is the second largest square in the world, after Tiananmen Square in Beijing. It is an enchanting place, with many historic structures of Islamic architecture and some of the finest mosaics contained in the many mosques that are interspersed between modern-day shops selling handicrafts and housewares. In Tehran, the nation's capital, a visit to the treasury, where the Crown Jewels from past monarchies are kept in all their magnificence and splendor, is a must. Let's not forget the Grand Bazaar in Tehran where, between bouts of shopping frenzy, I had the most delicious *ju je* (chicken) kebab sandwich ever. Shiraz is another fabled city. Iran's former capital and ancient metropolis, filled with museums and monuments, bazaars and eclectic eateries, is a must-visit as well.

Fundamentally speaking, I do not believe that people change per se. If history is a guide, traditions and cultures of ancient lands have a tendency of enduring. People make adjustments to suit the changing times and the circumstances, as the case may be. Modern day Persians or Iranians are a hospitable and congenial lot with a rich history, strong cultural traditions, and human values. Travelers to this ancient and inspirational land need to keep in mind that perception is not always reality.

The best *intelligence* is what we do with our leisure

—ERNEST BENN

ESCAPE FROM MILAN

I got trapped in Milan…in August….on a weekend. Italy's business and fashion capital has its charms, but once the shopping is done, and the obligatory visit to the Cathedral and the Monastery where Michelangelo painted the "Last Supper," you've pretty much run out of options.

It being the weekend, the hotel was deserted, and there wasn't even a swimming pool to cool off in. So I popped the big question to Mario, the friendly concierge: "Where do you go with your family on hot summer weekends?" "Stresa," came the answer, without hesitation, and he proceeded to give me detailed instructions on how to get there. I was saved.

The one-hour train ride (for less than US$20, return) to this pretty holiday town on Lake Maggiore was very pleasant. It's not only a fashionable resort area for the rich and famous, but is also gaining in popularity as a convention city. The promenades here rival some of the finest in the world, the French Riviera included. The walkways amongst the grand hotels (Negresco style) wind along the coastline and among luxurious villas. Surrounded by gardens brilliant with colorful and pretty flowers, they are absolutely delightful. This place is well worth a visit, yet most people overlook it. Thanks to my having nothing to do on a hot weekend day in Milan, I discovered Stresa.

But my escape from Milan underscores an age-old dilemma for hoteliers the world over: what to do about underutilized capacity in hotel restaurants and bars, especially on weekends. Barring being able to pick them up and move them to a better location, one might suggest that they stop building so many of them in the first place. For the ones that already exist, how about charging more reasonable prices and bringing back the fun? Give people real reasons to patronize the hotel and its restaurants and bars. This is a fairly simple idea – but hoteliers seem to have lost sight of the fact that leisure travelers aren't on a company business account.

Case in point: I got very stressed out one evening when I discovered I had been charged EU9.50 (equivalent to almost US$12) for a small bag of nuts I took from the in-room mini bar (or "hospitality bar" as they are euphemistically called) to satisfy a midnight craving. There was nothing hospitable about this episode. "I must have been nuts", I thought the next day. No wonder some people are afraid of using hotels these days, for fear of breaking the bank, and much like the not too hospitable mini bars, they can sometimes be more punishment than pleasure.

And you don't always have Stresa to escape to.

Forget not that the earth delights to feel your bare feet and the winds long to play with your hair

—Kahlil Gibran

SLEEPLESS IN SANTORINI

If you had to spend a sleepless night somewhere, where would it be?

It had rained the night before, and the earth was still baking in the heat of summer. I could smell the intoxicating earthly fumes, mixed with the cool ocean breeze coming through my open window. As I looked out, the moon was still casting its luminous rays on the vast ocean. The waters were still. So still a knife could cut through them. Soon it would be daybreak, and the start of a new day, on my favorite Cycladic island: Santorini, in the Mediterranean.

This Aegean island has the most extraordinary geology. Formed by a volcanic eruption in the 16th century BC, some say that Santorini is the location of the lost continent of Atlantis. Today, its inhabitants are a small community of adventurous dwellers, who live atop a huge mountain. Their population swells in the summer, when a few thousand visitors — including tourists like myself — make it their temporary home. I visited this island during the summer of 1972 for the first time. (The islanders here taught me to think in terms of summers, and not years.) It's a wonderful, enchanting and romantic place to visit and vacation.

My sleepless night on Santorini was eerily quiet. Even the distant barking of fighting dogs, which I had heard the night before, was nowhere to be heard. Suddenly, the silence was broken. A succession of rapid sounds — sometimes faint, sometimes strong — could be heard from a distance: Tak..Tak..Tak..Tak..Tak.. went the tired engine of a lone fisherman's boat as it struggled to reach the shore after an all night fishing expedition. These sounds bring back memories. They are rekindled each time I think of the place or hear its name, like a favorite song from the past.

This island of whitewashed houses, churches and monuments perched on the summit, the rich culture, the vast ocean around this mountainous region, the sound of the fishing boat, the smell of the earth – all these things evoke images and feelings of serenity and tranquility for me. They are reminders of another time, another me. Indelible memories are fondly remembered experiences. Priceless good times can last longer than more tangible things, even the physical beauty of a place. There are many beautiful islands in the world, and each one of them is unique in beauty and appeal. What sets them apart is not always clear. Like people, character and personality are part of the equation. It would be illogical to have to choose one over another as if they were a bunch of beauty contestants.

But there is no doubt in my mind that Santorini is a contender. It's not just the natural beauty (after all, next to people, encounters with natural beauty are the most potent), either. There's a certain quality to this place that can only be discovered late at night. So if you find yourself on this island in the summer, give yourself a wake up call when everyone else is sleeping. You'll see what I mean.

Health is the greatest gift, contentment the greatest wealth, faithfulness the best relationship

—Buddha

PLAYING DOCTOR

Final check? Passport, tickets, money. All packed and ready to go, then? Hang on — what about health precautions? And really, when it comes to health precautions for travelers, how much do we know?

Taking medical advice from a layman is dangerous, and I wouldn't normally presume to offer such advice. But I recently came across a nifty little booklet by Drs. Helen Oh and Chew Sukhai titled 'Health Guide for Travelers," which contains valuable information and helpful tips for prospective travelers.

The book is an easy read and contains many tips about immunization and various infectious diseases. Most, if not all, accidents can be prevented, because they involve human beings and human beings lack awareness, are generally forgetful, and are often careless. (If you nodded in agreement to at least one of the above, not to worry.... you are just a human being).

The advice given by the authors is quite basic: by maintaining a high level of awareness, one can avoid mishaps when traveling to exotic or unfamiliar places. The authors recommend eating cooked food and drinking bottled water and doing so in sufficient quantities to avoid dehydration. Frequent hand washing is also recommended. But it's not just new germs that fell travelers — many try to do too much in too short a time, in order to maximize their vacation experience. But this can backfire, instead lowering the body's resistance, and thus its ability to fight disease. The book offers advice for elderly travelers (take extra precautions, since a lower tolerance for heat in the elderly can lead to heatstroke) and Hajj pilgrims, as well as a list of websites for travel health.

Traveling can be a stressful experience even at the best of times. One needs to pay particular attention to the effects of jet lag, changes in weather, diet, motion sickness and the like. Planning ahead and knowing what to do and why is important if we want to stay healthy abroad. Otherwise, any preventable mishap will not only spoil our vacation, but also spoil it for those who might be traveling with us — and no one should have to play doctor on a trip.

All our knowledge has its origins in our perceptions

—Leonardo da Vinci

PERCEPTION IS ILLUSION
SEE WHAT I'M SAYING?

We often allow our travels to be put off by real and imagined threats. For instance, had I heeded reports about safety in Turkey, I would have never made the trip. Despite wails of caution on account of alleged terrorist attacks, my bags were packed.

Turkey is a country that presents fascinating contrasts. Antiquity and the past are juxtaposed with the contemporary, the familiar rubs up against the exotic, and through it all, visitors are treated like special guests. My experience was so captivating that I have been back twice since my first visit. But had I heeded the cautionary bulletins, I never would have gone — yet they can apply to practically every city in the world these days. So I prefer to ignore them, and listen to my inner self (but I do draw the line at visiting war zones). Life need not be put on hold. It should be experienced as a never-ending and exciting journey.

Most reports, generally speaking, tend to be exaggerated and sensationalized by the media. Perception is not always reality. Marketers like to say that a customer's perception is reality. This might be true in the commercial sense. Might this also apply to destinations as well as products? The answer, I suppose, depends on reliable information and the right assumptions. As management guru Peter Drucker used to say; "get the assumptions wrong and everything that follows will be wrong". Suffice it to say that we make assumptions all the time, and therefore it's important to have as many of the pertinent facts as possible before forming opinions. Otherwise, we are allowing fear to be our means of perception. And is not perception itself an illusion?

Alain de Botton recounts an insightful story in his book *The Art of Travel*, about a would-be traveler who engages in a pessimistic analysis of the difference between what he imagines about a place and what might occur when he reaches it. As the story goes, moments before embarking on the trip — the chance to turn his dream into reality — he is overcome by lassitude. The negative image he creates in his mind far outweighs the positive reasons he had considered when contemplating making the trip. Finally, he talks himself out of traveling entirely.

The author concludes that the reality of travel may not always be what we anticipate, but reality need not always be disappointing, just different. Perhaps it is time to put our money down on acceptance of what is, rather than expectation of what we perceive it could become. If one were to say, "nothing was as I had imagined it," it is surprising only if one considers what was imagined.

After my return, I came across an interesting piece by John Schwartz in the *New York Times*, about beginning a trip before a trip. "Read a book about the place before the trip begins," he says. As it happens, I try to do the same before I travel: on this particular trip to Turkey, I took along *The Song of Troy*, a wonderfully written book by Colleen McCullough about the Trojan wars.

It was an absolute joy to read this while in the setting where the story unfolds. For one, it put the entire experience, my illusions of reality, past and present, in an entirely different perspective. Do you see what I am saying?

Preserve the old and add the new

—BUDDHIST MONK, KYOTO

FUSION & PRESERVATION
IN KYOTO

I would not have believed it had I not seen it with my own eyes. According to the *Nihon Keizai Shimbun*, (Japan's equivalent to the *Wall Street Journal*), I was the first foreigner ever appointed to a position of hotel general manager in Kyoto. The year was 2001. A testament, perhaps, to the level of conservatism that permeates most aspects of social life in this fabled city; a city so steeped in Japanese culture it is probably the closest that one could get to the real Japan. Unlike other Japanese cities, the Americans preserved it for future generations by not bombing extensively during the Second World War. Kyoto is so charming that it might as well be a living museum; already several spots around this lovely former capital city have been selected for World Heritage honors.

Like most citizens of places with lineage, Kyoto-ites are fiercely proud of their history and their heritage. The city is famous for its handicrafts, electronics industry, fine universities and Buddhist temples. It was also the city of *Memoirs of a Geisha*, home to the Gion district and the fascinating Geisha or Geiko culture, as it is known locally. These unique artistes can be seen on the streets from time to time, although their way of life is slowly disappearing. Today, there are an estimated 300 geisha left in Kyoto, 1,500 in all of Japan – down from 80,000 during the decade prior to World War II. These days, geishas grace corporate social events with their musical and dance talents, and command hefty fees for doing so.

More than a hundred Buddhist temples dot Kyoto, but only seventeen are open to the public. They play a key role in every aspect of daily life: religious, social, political and economic. Their activities constitute big business for practically every local business and, in most cases, not maintaining good relations with them can have devastating financial consequences. Naturally, I visited several Buddhist temples with a group of associates to present my credentials and to solicit support for future business.

Whilst partaking in the tea ceremony at one of the temples, our host, the temple's head monk (who had apparently read the piece about my appointment in the newspaper) asked me a rather simple, yet loaded question (never underestimate the wisdom of a Buddhist monk). "And what are you going to do with Kyoto's 111-year-old hotel?" he politely asked. I took advantage of the priestly surroundings to contemplate the question. The reason was simple: I needed time to think the question through. Under normal circumstances, a canned corporate response would have sufficed. Not this time, not in this place and not for this particular questioner. The word "harmony" came to mind. "We shall ensure that tradition and modernity coexist in harmony with everything we do," I said. "And what does this mean?" he promptly asked. This type of conversational badminton went on for quite a while. "Harmonizing tradition with modernity is an interesting thought," he concluded at one point, "but you need not think of it in terms of mixing the old with the new, as is often the case. No need to destroy the old by mixing with the new to create something new. Preserve the old and add the new."

This insightful, yet simple idea, as insightful ideas go, was a theme we often discussed, as we were becoming friends. As time went on, I came to appreciate our discussions for helping me understand the new culture and to cope with managerial tasks in this new setting. The notion, for instance, that good management transcends culture. And why fusion cuisine disagrees with my palate.

Never go back to where you were once happy

for it will never be the same

—CHINESE SAYING

GOING BACK

When asked where he came from, Socrates did not say "from Athens", but "from the world". It's a sentiment familiar to many in the modern world, but Socrates was talking more about attitude than altitude. The kind of attitude that is born from travel.

Changing environment, even for a few days, can be very uplifting. I visited a well-known resort recently in Macau. A resort is a place where people go to repose, renew and rejuvenate, and this particular resort does this especially well, thanks to Akram, the General Manager and his well-trained staff who go out of their way to please customers. After all, fancy designs, interiors and glitzy finishes can be easily reproduced, but caring and friendly service is a priceless thing.

And this is what really makes the difference: five-star people delivering five-star service on a consistent basis. Service may be intangible, but it is what most people remember and appreciate. According to studies, patrons generally remember the treatment they receive, and the people involved even more so than the resort's physical attributes. Would I choose to return if Akram and others in his team had moved on, as is often the case in the hotel trade? Maybe not, because I don't think it would be the same: still good service, perhaps, but it wouldn't be the same. Therefore, I shall resort (no pun intended) to remembering the good time I had at the resort and the good people that made it happen. Next time, I will most likely visit another resort for, in reality, what are my chances of finding the same happiness in the same place?

The Chinese have a saying; 'never go back to where you were once happy for it will never be the same." I imagine this to mean both physically and psychologically. Like most people, I often find myself thinking of the past and going back, as it were, to people, and places, real or imagined. What might make one want to go back to a place or a time are feelings of genuine welcome and true appreciation, or perhaps to a place where one is made to feel the most alive with joy and utter contentment. The longing to go back is understandable, but if you go back, don't expect it to be the same.

In life, as with travel, lowering one's expectations, and raising one's acceptance levels of others invariably increases the chances for pleasant surprise, increased satisfaction and true fulfillment. Try it the next time.

Hope Forever

Even if it is late it's not too late
for miracles-for hope

For hope, part aberration, part inspiration

We are everywhere, somewhere, and nowhere

Forever is in every waking new day

In every happy moment

Live forever, for the moment

—PETER ALATSAS

SHORT BREAKS & TAKES

Whilst on assignment in Bandar Seri Begawan, the capital of Brunei Darussalam, I took a short break to visit exotic India. Brunei is a small country of roughly 300,000 mostly Malay inhabitants, and because of its small size, lack of cosmopolitanism and close proximity to more exciting capitals, escaping to some "other place" for a short break was a common practice for most expatriates. This oil rich sultanate is not in the Middle East, as some might easily assume, but on the island of Borneo in South East Asia.

The journey by road from New Delhi to Agra, the one time seat of the Mugal Empire, was an experience unlike any I have ever had. Our four door black sedan was surprisingly comfortable and reasonably clean with white cotton laced seat covers. Though we were kept amused and entertained by the hospitable and unabashedly talkative driver he, nevertheless, kept us on edge, bent as he was on speeding, even though we had told him we were in no particular hurry. He must have been a kamikaze in a previous life. We were on a narrow stretch of road with single two-way traffic lanes and white knuckling it most of the time, trying to brace ourselves from being catapulted into some unsuspecting farmer's yoke. Our driver was the equivalent of a sprinter gone amok on the track, passing as many cars, trucks, buses, tractors, cows, bicycles, rickshaws, and people as he could. On several occasions we felt as though we were going to meet our maker; fortunately, the grim reaper had taken the day off.

Somehow, this charming maniacal driver managed to survive the ordeal along with the rest of us.

Even with the windows closed, the smell of animal dung (which is used as cooking fuel) permeated throughout adding, in a rather bizarre way, a crescendo to the adventure. It was especially potent in the late evening hours, when cooking for supper was at its peak. We were on our way to the fabled white marble tomb, the Taj Mahal. Seeing this majestic monument to love was a highly emotional experience in every way. So much so that we decided to name our soon-to-be-born son Jahan, after the Mugal Emperor Shah Jahan, the man who built the Taj Mahal as a monument for his second wife Mumtaz Mahal, who was, like his mother, a very beautiful Muslim Persian princess. What started out as a routine break turned out to be a most memorable and enlightening experience, despite the sometimes real and sometimes imagined risks along the way.

Fast-forward several years on. Whilst on assignment in Kyoto, Japan, I found myself at the quaint and very enchanting Kodai-Ji Zen temple during the "sakura" (cherry blossom) season. Inspired by its natural setting, history, elegance and style, I could not help but recall the magnificence of the Taj Mahal. And as it turns out, this temple was another monument to love. The incredibly beautiful temple, with gardens to match, was built by Kitano Mandokoro, and dedicated to her husband, Toyotomi Hideyoshi, the great Samurai warrior who unified Japan almost five centuries ago. Kitano had built the temple so that she could pray for the repose of his soul.

Cherry blossoms abound in the temple gardens. They are affectionately known as the "wabisabi" of Japanese aestheticism. The Japanese adore these gorgeous, fragile blossoms that appear once a year and last for about a week. The Japanese passion for cherry blossoms is not just a response to their grace and beauty. The sakura also reminds them, as the temple literature proclaims, "…of the fertility of life, evoking empathy with all living things that only have a limited life span, as well as a sense of admiration for a noble ending, like life and death." This is why the Japanese have associated cherry blossoms with their views of life and death – life is beautiful and short, like the cherry blossoms, and one should enjoy each day to the fullest.

Most recently, while on assignment in Shanghai, I took a short break in Sanya, China's premier resort destination and the self-proclaimed; "Hawaii of China". (A slice of Hawaii is more apt, in my estimation). Recalling the preceding events and inspired by their fond memories over the years, I took pen to paper and synthesized the borrowed words in the poem on page 57, "Hope Forever".

Mystras

Ghost city of solitude
— memories of ruin

Dilapidated walls in decay
— refuse of time

Face of wrinkled age
— beauty in ruin

—PETER ALATSAS

FINDING MYSTRAS

The picturesque medieval city of Mystras lies at the foot of the mountain where the ancient Spartans discarded babies thought too weak to become warriors. This hill-top city was a onetime capital of the despotate of Morea (modern day Peloponnesus), which thrived as a political, economic, religious and cultural center for almost two centuries (1262-1460). The last vestiges of the Byzantine Empire began to unravel with the fall of Constantinople (modern day Istanbul) in 1453. Shortly afterwards, Mystras was handed over to the Ottomans. Constantine, the last Byzantine Emperor, lived here before the fall of his mighty empire. Somehow, this place stirs the imagination and evokes images of majesty, romance and life struggle. These days, it lies in ruins, and there is much to experience. As one historian put it: "the city is solitary and elegant and free to meditate at its own tempo". He's right: the 6-kilometer bus ride from modern day Sparta will transport you back to the 14th century.

The imposing church and monastery of Pantanassa is inhabited by a handful of nuns, a succession of whom has made it their temporary home on earth for centuries. As with so many things ancient, there are many traditions associated with Pantanassa – for example, students etch their names on the dilapidated church walls for good luck. I was one of those students, but try as I might, I could not find my name among the multitude that were etched on the church walls. It was nowhere to be found. I wanted so much to find it, and be reminded of my carefree days.

This place is a stark reminder of the last days of the Byzantine Empire, and of a Europe in transition — the renaissance and enlightenment. But the once-stately homes of royalty and aristocrats are not as well preserved as the places of worship. Charming Byzantine churches, with their impressive, eye-catching mosaics, dot the once-narrow streets that have become pathways over time. Aromatic flora and fauna cover these pathways, and on hot summer days, their fragrance is positively intoxicating.

Summer – the early summer morning hours – is especially peaceful at Pantanassa. If it were not for the chirping birds and the odd donkey growl, I might have been alone with the ruins. The huge tree, just below the monastery, in whose shade I used to sit and do schoolwork, was still there. So were the nuns. I would always pay them a visit before heading back to the city. I always looked forward to their offer of cookies and a cordial made from wild sour cherries mixed with iced water. Sadly, though, I did not recognize any of the nuns, and neither did they recognize me. Though I tried hard to retrieve myself from their age-old memories, nothing I said jolted them. Small comfort that just as in the past, they offered their visitor libation, bid him farewell and Godspeed. I tried hard to hold back tears as I gulped it down. Having struck out twice, once with my name and once with the nuns, I headed down the hill.

Another equally enchanting place I used to frequent was Monemvasia. This medieval town is also perched on a hillside, only this one is surrounded by the deepest, bluest Mediterranean waters. If not for the causeway connecting it with the mainland it would have been an island. This pretty place offers rich history and period architecture, stunning vistas and sunsets, and is just under an hour's drive from Sparta. The road snakes around quaint little towns and villages, making the journey along the way very pleasant, peaceful and memorable, scenic and inspirational — as all journeys should be.

Man:
A being in search of meaning

—PLATO

PARTS UNKNOWN

People ask me where I'm from, but what they really want to know is where I was born.

Whilst serving in Jeddah, Saudi Arabia, I met a well-traveled and rather sophisticated Saudi man who looked like a Bedouin. He was, in many ways, the embodiment of this hospitable, exotic and paradoxical land. For some unknown reason, he was bent on finding the origins of my last name. After several months of searching, he concluded that my last name had its origins in Yemen. Imagine my surprise. Several years later, in a bookstore in London, the gentle man behind the cash register, after gazing at the books I was about to purchase, announced, "I have just the book for you," before going off to find it. Reappearing before anyone in the queue lost patience, he produced a book written by the very accomplished travel writer Patrick Leigh Fermor called *Mani: Travels in the Southern Peloponnese*.

The book traces Fermor's travels with his wife through the fabled Mani and the surrounding areas. Many of the places he mentions in this book were eerily familiar from my traveling days as a teenager. For centuries, this has been unforgiving territory. The terrain, though impressive, is as rugged as its fiercely patriotic inhabitants. Invaders over the centuries have either given up trying to invade or were just simply not interested in this place at all, thanks to all of the unfavorable publicity. Clan rivalries and intense family feuding, for reasons mostly of "honor", would last for decades, resulting in the deaths of many men. Violent death was so common that newborn boys were called "guns" rather than sons. Until recent times, no central government was ever able to properly control or to administer this unusual region.

It is not unusual to connect emotionally with places and people when traveling. Perhaps it is because certain cultures overlap in rather peculiar and inexplicable ways. Perhaps it is merely Providence — or is it that we are all "made of the same stock," so to speak, and respond to the same things?

But back to Fermor's book, which, for me, was more than just a good travel read. In it, I discovered that my last name had its origins in a picturesque town that lies a few kilometers from where I was born. Fermor takes an in depth look at the original settlers, who were predominantly Jewish leather merchants — yet he is unable to conclude, with any degree of certainty, the true origins of the present day dwellers.

No surprises there: tracing one's lineage is challenging enough, even in the best of circumstances. Some people travel at length and spare no expense to find their roots. The challenge, if you like, is how to separate fact from fiction. This is a dilemma that has preoccupied historians since time immemorial, and will continue to do so for centuries more.

My rather crude and elementary foray into the artful science of heritage discovery left me with the following conclusion: I hail from some parts known and some parts unknown — in a way, I got lost somewhere between origin and original. Didn't we all? What really matters is how we go about living and enjoying life in all its cosmic bliss rather than dwelling on where we are from or where we were born. And wouldn't it be nice if no one ever pops the question — or any of its myriad variations — again.

One who rises, rises of himself
One who falls, falls of himself

—Ni Bittsu

IMAGINE PEACE IN
THE MIDDLE EAST

Shanghai might be the most talked about city in the world, but Dubai is reportedly the world's fastest growing. Certainly, it has ambition: Dubai is building the world's largest international airport. Operational by the end of 2007, it will be twice the size of Hong Kong island. According to recent reports, the new Dubai World Central airport will have six runways, and be able to handle 120 million passengers. Once operational, it will have almost double London Heathrow's current handling capacity. The project, which includes a self-contained "smart city" with the latest in technology, modern life style dwellings, shops, theaters and museums, is destined to be an urban planning masterpiece.

Despite the political unrest in this area, Israel and many of the Gulf States have seen a dramatic rise in tourism arrivals in recent years. The Middle East continues to be the fastest growing region in terms of air passenger traffic and the fourth most visited area in the world.

Aside from the well-publicized mega projects and construction-related activity in Dubai, the Arabian Peninsula has seen unprecedented growth over the past five years in new hotel development as well. Almost 100 new hotels have either opened or are in the planning stages for opening over the next five years. Most of these luxury hotels will open in Dubai and Doha. Over the past two years, this region has outperformed both Asia and Europe in terms of hotel revenue generated on a per room available basis (or REVPAR, an industry standard that measures effectiveness in maximizing top line growth). If present trends continue, the Middle East region will surpass the U.S. in REVPAR by the end of the decade.

Imagine if there was peace in the Middle East? A few years back, my company sent me on assignment to Doha. Doha? I was skeptical, but my skepticism quickly turned into optimism. It became quite evident that this tiny emirate (one-third the size of Belgium) with a population of just under one million was going to rival Dubai — the self proclaimed commercial "powerhouse" of the Middle East. It was only a matter of when. Much like in Shanghai these days, cranes, not stars, dotted the Qatari sky, and energy and optimism were everywhere. This is still the case, according to recent reports, and this small emirate has grand plans to triple its tourist arrivals to 1.4 million in the next two years. This is just one small example — imagine the untapped potential of this exotic region. Imagine, if there was peace in the Middle East.

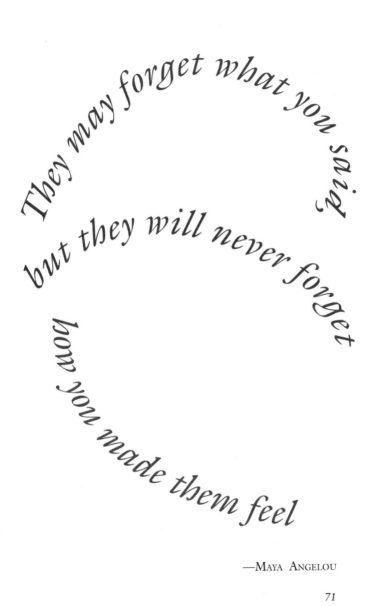

They may forget what you said, but they will never forget how you made them feel

—MAYA ANGELOU

MORE THAN JUST A MUSEUM

Liuligongfang is the name of a remarkable new museum in Shanghai that morphs into a wine bar for beautiful, artsy people and other sophisticates in the evening.

Situated adjacent to the trendy Xintiandi area, the exterior façade is imposing: simple, yet grand. Aside from a gigantic sculpted "Mudan" flower, (China's national flower), which protrudes elegantly from its exterior wall, there are no signs marking the building. No need to. This place is a landmark, thanks to its Zen-like architecture and inspirational interior design, and for the exquisite exhibits of crystal glass objects and jewellery for which Liuligongfang is renowned. Not to mention its cachet as a late-night venue for an after-dinner drink in the sensually soothing, relaxing and elegant surroundings with terraces and pretty views of the city skyline.

My mystical journey around the dimly lit passageways featuring objects of art on display was augmented by sensuous sounds and lighting. The use of lighting in particular has been elevated to a new level, which evoked a temple-like atmosphere at different points and stages of my tour. As I moved from section to section with Victoria, the congenial representative, I felt as if I was being transported to another place and another time. Even the washrooms have been elevated to an art form, featuring wall to wall cut glass interiors reflecting the fine fittings and colorful objects of art within. It made me feel that I was part of the interior as well as the experience.

This modern palace of exquisite art-cum-place of worship and enjoyment has to be seen. It has been conceived by a group of immensely talented people

There is an uplifting and temple-like, spiritual atmosphere that one feels, thanks to its aesthetic attention to every detail that touches all the senses as well as the innovative and creative interior. The minute I walked out, I felt the mental gyrations of re-entry into the real world and back to sizzling Shanghai. This beautiful place was created by a group of exceptionally gifted and talented artists with a passion for excellence and an unconditional love for Chinese art and culture. And it shows.

Liuligongfang is a most welcome addition to the city's rich cultural life. They have proven, in their own inimitable way, that simplicity is both elegance and luxury.

What the gentleman seeks,
he seeks within himself;
What the small man seeks,
he seeks in others

—Confucius

GOING SOLO

Picture the all-too-familiar scene of the lonely diner, struggling to read a book in a dimly lit restaurant, all the while desperately trying to convey the impression "I'm not alone". Despite the conveniences and new age attitudes, some people continue to feel uncomfortable with the idea of dining, traveling or vacationing alone. Reasons range from concerns about safety to a need for companionship – even economizing.

I have noticed people dining on their own, or in the company of a good read – and although I've never seen anyone dine with a pet, this is an idea whose time may have come. Pet-friendly programs are a growth trend in the hotel and restaurant business, one that is destined to go mainstream. Catering for pets is more or less the same as catering for people, and pet lovers should never have to be solo.

Going it alone used to mean having no fun. Not anymore. Fodor's Travel publications recently surveyed over 1,000 Americans, and discovered that in the last three years, four in 10 Americans actually preferred to travel or vacation alone for more than two nights. Many baby boomers, according to the same study, are newly divorced, widowed, or are simply single. About 80 percent of the respondents agree that traveling alone for pleasure would allow them the freedom to do what they want, when they want to do it. 71 percent feel that traveling alone would be a fun way to meet new people. Still, both male and female respondents agreed that it was easier for a man than for a woman, and that for most women, there was still a stigma to traveling alone, and more so, dining alone. To a large extent, this helps explain the popularity of cruises and spas, considered perfect options for solo travelers, since they offer an all-inclusive price deal and the choice of going solo or with a group.

The study concludes that as Americans become more mobile and single women overcome the stigma of going solo, new growth opportunities in products and services catering to their specific needs are on the horizon. Both these developments – mobility and single women – have universal application in the sense that both are phenomena of the new age, and the findings mentioned above can reasonably apply the world over. Travel and related services, by their very natures, are a global business. Together with the impetus from globalization, going solo or not, it is a big business as well.

It is not good for all you wish to be fulfilled;

through sickness you recognize

the value of health,

through evil the value of good,

through hunger, satisfaction,

through exertion, the value of rest.

—HERACLITUS

GIVE THEM A BETTER SEAT

I was amused when, post 9-11, major airlines began providing plastic knives and metal forks (or vice-versa) with in-flight meals. Really, did they think this would stop someone who was determined to do violence? I was recently vindicated by an incident where a 50-year-old passenger, flying from Bangkok to Sydney on a major Asian carrier, was stabbed in the neck with a fork. The injuries sustained were of a minor nature, and after being treated in Sydney, he is now safely back at home.

The 22-year-old man had stabbed him over a seating dispute. Violence may be inexcusable, but anyone who has experienced the cramped, crummy seats in economy class can understand the frustrations. No wonder some people lose it!

Why airlines have not redesigned the seats in economy to make them more user-friendly and less bulky, with emphasis on providing more comfort and space, is beyond me. The seats in economy have looked and felt the same for decades.

Many of the major carriers are cutting the price of business fares, which have traditionally subsidized leisure travelers' fares. This means that the price of economy class seats will go up in the months and years ahead, perhaps staying up, while the price of business class seats will go down, as airlines struggle with profitability. All the more reason why better quality seating is required in economy class — which some airlines euphemistically call "hospitality" class. There is nothing hospitable about being stuck in a heinous yoga position for hours, especially on a long-haul trans-Pacific flight.

The stabbing itself is another story. It is completely inappropriate behavior, whatever the underlying reason. On the other hand, how much safety protection is enough before we reach a level of absurdity? Or was this a PR campaign by the airlines for the sake of perceived cabin safety? The idea isn't so bad. Some might even argue that the initiative is better than none at all. In the wrong hands, a plastic fork or knife is likely to cause more or less the same amount of damage. Almost anything can be used as a lethal weapon these days. Is prevention the way to go about treating irate passengers before they go amok? Give them a better seat, I say.

A tourist is someone who travels to see things that are different and then complains when they aren't the same

—Anonymous

TIDBITS OF WISDOM — OR FOLLY?

Over the years, I have come across some rather bizarre episodes and anecdotes about travel. Let's face it: everyone has a story to tell after a trip, and as the old saying goes, "everyone has something to contribute – even broken clocks get the time right twice a day."

In the unlikely event that you don't have a story to tell friends after a trip, here are some eminently retail-able signs from hotels that might inspire you to recall your own … or at the very least, provide some fodder.

In an Acupulco hotel: "The manager has personally passed all the water served here."

In a Paris hotel elevator: "Please leave your values at the front desk."

In a Vienna hotel: "In case of fire, do your utmost to alarm the hotel porter."

On a Moscow hotel door: "If this is your first visit, you are welcome to it."

In an Athens hotel: "Visitors are expected to complain at the office from 9am to 11am daily."

In a hotel in Tokyo: "Is forbidden to steal hotel towels please. If you are not person to do such thing, please do not read notice."

In a hotel in Yokohama: "You are expected to take advantage of the Chambermaid."

In a Zurich hotel: "Because of the impropriety of entertaining guests of the opposite sex in the bedroom, it is suggested that the lobby is used for this purpose."

And it's not just hotels, either. Here's an interesting sign, spotted across the road from a Russian Orthodox Monastery: "You are welcome to visit the cemetery where famous Russian composers, artists and writers are buried daily except Thursday."

THE BUSINESS
OF LIFE

"No man is a failure who is enjoying life."

—WILLIAM FAULKNER

*"Life can only be understood backwards,
but must be lived forwards."*

—SOREN KIERKEGARD

The less of routine, the more of life

—A.B. Alcott

ORDER & DISORDER
IN THE TOWN SQUARE

Town squares are a big part of European culture. In Greece, they are the center of life in virtually every city and village, favorite gathering spots for the community. This is as true in Athens, where scores of cafes dot the streets, as it is in the small villages. In this amazing country, where antiquity and modernity coexist in harmony, coffee culture — along with football and national lotteries — is a daily ritual.

I decided to participate at an Athens street side café, sipping coffee and watching the world go by. Needless to say, I joined the many other enthusiasts (or hedonists, as the Athenians might say), who were engaged in the same. It didn't harm me a bit. Especially as I was under the sunny azure skies and cool gentle breezes that typify most days of the year in this exotic land. It was on one such day that a middle-aged man, sitting at the table next to me, interrupted my concentration. He politely introduced himself as a dentist from Germany.

"I have been coming to Athens every year for many years, and I love to watch the crowds in the streets. Ever wonder where these people are coming from and where they are going?" he asked.

"No," I admitted, "but most major cities are busy these days." (Hardly a profound statement, but it was the best I could do on short notice.) "There is something about this city — not that it doesn't work, mind you – but there is a sense of chaos and disorder that relaxes me."

"How can disorder relax you? Isn't your thinking a contradiction in terms?" I asked.

"Maybe," came the reply, "but do you know what the Ancient Greeks used to say? 'There is order in disorder'. Where I come from there is too much order, and not enough disorder," he complained.

This symposium-like encounter gave me a renewed sense and appreciation for the noble virtues of patience and tolerance. Traveling the globe as a mercenary of business I have come to realize that both of these virtues are essential ingredients for modern day peaceful and cultural co-existence. As for my new-found German friend, I reckon he is destined to happily continue with his visits to Athens for many more years to rejuvenate and rediscover the therapeutic qualities of chaos.

The idea or notion of striving to keep things in order and under control — our cities, ourselves and the people around us — all of the time can cause a great deal of unnecessary strain. Thriving on orderly chaos (if there is such a thing) and practicing conscious aimlessness (if one can perfect the art) can be a source of great satisfaction and discovery.

If

If you turn your back on your destiny
Look for the other side of the mountain
You might start anew.

If you turn your back on love
Look for the other side of your heart
You might find it.

If love is destiny, to love
What is loved belongs to someone else.

If giving is receiving, to love
We love as much as we are loved
-and sometimes more

—PETER ALATSAS
AT MOUNT ATHOS
SEPTEMBER 3, 2005

LINKED IN HUMANITY

Mount Athos, the oldest monastic republic in existence, is located on the Athos peninsula in Northern Greece, 2,033 feet above sea level. Its history goes back to the 5th century BC, but the monastic communities here weren't officially established until 963. Today, Mount Athos is an autonomous region or state within the Greek state.

I asked a monk here why he had chosen the life of a hermit. "To be closer to God," was his simple and immediate response. He was also quick to point out that there are many misconceptions, and considerable ignorance, about monastic life. "It is hard work, and requires intense dedication. Most people are under the impression that men come here to escape organized life or problems and tragedies. Yes, there are a few who arrive with this notion, but they usually don't last too long."

It takes at least three years to become a monk. A higher calling and deep personal commitment are prerequisites. The Greek word for monk is "Mona-hos" which literally translated means, "to be alone" – or, if you are in a "Monastery", alone with God.

There are over 2,000 monks and 20 monasteries at Mount Athos, 16 of which are Greek. (The others are Russian, Bulgarian, Lebanese and Serbian.) All follow the Eastern Christian Orthodox tradition.

Up to 100 men of all faiths are welcomed each day as visitors. (Only men: since the 10th century, only men have been permitted on the mountain.) They can stay overnight, for up to four nights, and are welcome to participate in the daily routines if they wish. They are fed and housed at no cost. A visitor's permit or visa is required for entry and one needs to get in line early. The wait can sometimes take months.

The monastery buildings, the natural beauty, the peacefulness and the serenity were all so impressive — but what impressed me the most was the caliber of the monks. These gentlemen had come from all walks of life: doctors, lawyers, architects, computer programmers and the like. Their perspectives on issues, and on life in general, were most enlightening.

After a warm welcome at the pier on the day of my arrival, I was offered a delicious meal prepared by my greeter, and afterwards shown to a small room to rest for a while. "You must be tired from your journey. I will wake you up when it is time," he said, as closing the door of my tiny room, so small that it barely fit the single bed inside. The room's most distinguishing feature was a small window overlooking the tranquil, turquoise waters of the Mediterranean and an almost invisible horizon against the background of a cloudless deep blue sky. If there was ever a proper definition for "breathtaking," this was it. I was more tired from the heat of summer than the journey itself, and gladly placed myself horizontally to rest as instructed. My ears were buzzing from the silence — a kind of deafening silence that prevented me from napping for some time. Finally, exhausted by the 'Sounds of Silence', I succumbed for a few hours.

Monks sleep for eight hours, pray for eight hours, and work and rest (mostly read) for the rest of the time. Their diet consists mainly of fruits, vegetables olive oil and cheese, with fish once a week. There are no banquets here — they eat enough to survive.

I am not sure if my newfound friends would approve of me writing about my brief stay. They are discreet, and, as my host pointed out during one of our many informative chats, "this is not a place for tourists". Even so, I had an overwhelming desire to honor these extraordinary men, if for no other reason than to express my gratitude for the chance to meet and talk with them, and for their unconditional hospitality.

On the ship back to organized life, I often looked back at Mount Athos. Whilst leaning on the railing under the scorching sun, I could see the community I had just visited slowly disappearing from view. The dwellings, slowly giving in to the horizon, appeared as if they were hanging from the side of the huge mountain, becoming tiny specks as the boat moved farther and farther away, until all I could see was the profile of a mountain rising from inside the vast ocean. My thoughts were mainly about there being more similarities than differences between the peoples of the world and of the importance and value of tolerance and understanding — how we are all linked in humanity and in cosmic destiny on this shared planet.

Candles

The days of the future stand before us
Like a row of little lighted candles-
Gold and warm and lively little candles.
The days past remain behind.
A sad line of snuffed out candles;
The nearest are still smoking,
Cold candles, bent and melted.
I don't want to see them;
the sight of them hurts me,
And it hurts me to remember their first light,
I look in front of my lighted candles,
I don't want to turn around and see and tremble
At how fast the dark line is growing,
How fast the snuffed out candles are multiplying.

—CAVAFY

THE JOURNEY WITHIN

On a recent trip from Hong Kong to Europe, a friend of mine was asked if he had anything to declare at the customs counter. "No, I do not," he told the customs official. Unconvinced, the official asked him to open his suitcase, and as he was about to peek into his toiletry bag (where several high quality counterfeit watches had been stashed), my friend gently leaned over the counter in an obvious effort to obscure the official from his children, and pleaded: "If you open it you will spoil my children's Christmas." After pondering the situation for a few seconds, the official decided to wave the family through, wishing them a 'Merry Christmas'.

Bending the rules to make some kids happy was a lovely gesture, very much in keeping with the spirit of Christmas. In the grand scheme of things, imagine how the world would function – and malfunction — if rules were followed to the letter. It is natural to bend rules for good reason from time to time. As the saying goes: "a tree has to bend with the wind, otherwise it snaps".

Just as rules need to bend sometimes, so the truth is often a shade of grey, rather than black or white, as in this philosophical exchange between father and son: "Does Father Christmas exist?" asks the boy. "Do you want him to?" asks the father. "Yes I do", replies the boy. "Then he exists," says his father.

Philosophical interpretations aside, parents, for some kids, tend to exist in the abstract much like Father Christmas because they are often away from home. Quality time is still the buzzword. If peace begins at home, as most faiths would have us believe, then striking a balance is an imperative.

Of course, there are countless perspectives on the meaning of life and the essence of time. Happiness, I like to think, features prominently in every equation. As Ralph Waldo Emerson wrote, "What lies behind us and lies before us are small matters to what lies within us."

All the water in the world
However hard it tried,
Could never, never sink a ship
Unless it got inside.

All the evil in the world,
The wickedness and sin,
Can never sink your soul's fair craft
unless you let it in.

All the hardships of this world,
Might wear you pretty thin,
But they won't hurt you, one least bit...
Unless you let them in.

—ANONYMOUS

GETTING TO YOU

People will say one thing — and do another. They are also quick to dispense priceless pearls of wisdom – and then fail to heed them. How many times do we hear people utter what is probably the most overused cliché: "Life is short," and yet do almost everything to make the least of their short life.

People ask me when and where I'm going to retire. Retire to what, I ponder. I like to feel that I'm in a constant state of retirement, for as long as I can travel, and for as long as I can think, and practice the art of working to live, and not living to work. I try my level best to make the most of every travel opportunity by going with the attitude that I might never come back to that particular place again, so why not make the most of it, in every way possible? Although I stick to a budget, and what I can afford, cost does not really enter my mind in the sense that it does not fuel or drive my enthusiasm. I simply refuse to let such matters get to me.

The pursuit of happiness for some people seems elusive, while for others it is a common occurrence. In either case our mood, to a large extent, is determined by our attitude and state of mind as well as the choices we make in our life. Good choices mean good results and pleasant memories; bad choices mean bad results and unpleasant memories. But reliving the past from the depths of our memory can easily confuse a person. What's real and what's imagined becomes blurred. Repeat a lie or imagine something often enough, and after a while, it becomes the truth or the reality.

Research has shown that when we reminisce about the past, it is often to recall unpleasant or bad memories as opposed to pleasant or good ones. In this context, most people I know choose to live in the past — to recall mishaps and unpleasantness rather than learning from the past by recalling lessons learned and happy occasions. This is easier said than done, but not impossible, providing one has a positive mental attitude. Consider also, that change is a constant, and how we are changing is far more important than who we were, and even who we are.

It is not the strongest of the species

that survives,

nor the most intelligent that survives.

It is the one that is most adaptable to change.

—CHARLES DARWIN

AWAY FROM HOME

A 20-year-old Australian man of Chinese origin took his own life recently in Sydney, after the restaurant he worked for accused him of stealing a dinner roll. Working in an alien culture took its toll on this unfortunate fellow, who was unable to make the necessary adjustments and cope.

According to his co-workers, the young man ate a dinner roll at the start of his shift and management then suspended him for stealing, with five days without pay. According to one of his co-workers, (who was present at the time), "the young man explained that he took the bread roll because he was hungry, but the manager insisted that it was stealing."

The young man apparently chose to end his life rather than suffer the humiliation of an investigation that would have ultimately become known to his parents and friends back home in Shanghai.

Anecdotal evidence suggests that most people don't really assimilate to a new environment. Instead, they adapt to various degrees. Some are savvier than others when it comes to culture shock. Those who are unable or unwilling to make the necessary adjustments risk withering away in agony, going from one mental collision to another. Any new place is unfamiliar, and will remain as such, unless one makes the necessary sacrifices, concessions and adjustments. Everything is difficult before it becomes easy. Arriving at a new airport for the first time is scary for most people. Being away from home, family, friends and familiar surroundings is also scary — to the extent one is willing to deal effectively with the complexities of change and the unfamiliar.

I sympathize with the deep hurt of the young Chinese Australian, wrongly accused of something he didn't do. Those who have had similar experiences will relate to this incident with empathy, while those who have not may choose to dismiss this tragic incident as a "work environment relations" problem.

Good management transcends culture. Respecting and managing differences is both an attitude and a skill. However, it is easier to teach skills than attitude. In fact, teaching attitude is like trying to teach someone personality. You either have it, or you don't. (Seems the manager in this story didn't have it.)

For Asians, "face"— integrity and reputation — is a serious matter. Tampering with reputation and credibility is a severe wrongdoing, especially if you hail from an ancient and traditional society, such as China's.

As God disposes man laughs or weeps.

—Sophocles

By nature,
all men are pretty much alike;
it is by custom and habit
that they are set apart.

—Confucius

SOPHOCLES & LAO SHE

Whilst living in Japan, I had the chance to enjoy Sophocles' ancient tragedy, 'Antigone", performed by a troupe from the National Theatre of Greece to a mostly Japanese audience. And I had the chance to rediscover the modern day relevance of this 2,500-year-old masterpiece.

I saw this play for the first time as a teenager. This time around, I found it considerably more meaningful, as I kept drawing parallels between what was happening on the stage before me — and on the world political stage. The main message of the play, after all, is that tragedies are created by people.

Antigone is forced to choose between her conscience and the rule of law, while King Creon is forced to defend the state and its laws from real and imagined threats. Both go to extremes to defend their respective positions with considerable pathos (as one would expect from a Greek tragedy). Both believe they are right and are highly convincing, vigorous and stubborn in approach and argument. Sadly though, in the end, reason and humanity do not prevail, for both remain intransigent — determined to act on principle alone, leading to the tragic deaths of innocent people, great suffering and unhappiness. The consequences of their actions make them both responsible for these dire outcomes. Ultimately, both are villains.

I was probably one of a handful in the audience that was able to enjoy the play, which was staged in Greek, without having to rent earphones for simultaneous translation. I was lucky – but I am less fortunate with the Shanghai stage.

Shanghai has many fine Chinese plays to offer, but as a non-Mandarin speaker, I am reliant on the English subtitles screened on video prompts on either side of the stage. Watching with one eye on the subtitles and one eye on the stage is not the ideal way to see a play – but it's better than nothing. Nothing – that is, no English translation – was available for "The Crescent Moon", Lao She's play about the lives of a mother and daughter confronting poverty and prostitution in the 1930s. I desperately wanted to see it, but without English translation, it was impossible. I felt culturally starved.

Wouldn't it be wonderful if simultaneous translation were made available rather than having to read off of those intoxicating video prompts whilst trying to enjoy a play? A simple idea, but that could also help catapult Shanghai onto the world stage as a true theater hub. What a great way to help boost tourism in the city, as well.

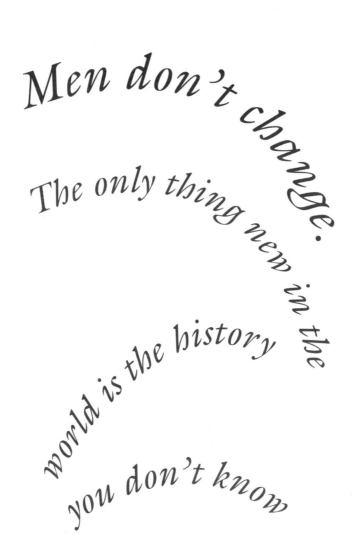

Men don't change. The only thing new in the world is the history you don't know

—HARRY S. TRUMAN

MEETING IN CYBERSPACE

As a boy, I remember the thrill of watching television for the first time in the 1950s. We were the first family on Ivy Street to have one. Needless to say, my stable of friends grew exponentially. The buzz in those days was that television would replace movie theaters. It didn't quite happen. Although there are fewer theaters today than there were before the advent of commercial television, they have not altogether disappeared, as we know. Many people still prefer to see movies on the big screen for the sheer enjoyment, intrinsic value and satisfaction of socializing in the process. Going to the movies, like going to a football game, is very appealing, as popular as ever, and destined to survive the passage of time.

A couple of decades ago, the world was introduced to commercial video-conferencing and the promise that businesspeople would save millions on travel expenses (ostensibly because companies could have their people conduct most, if not all their meetings, on television — anywhere and anytime, as the internet parlance goes. "Why travel when people can meet in cyberspace?" they said.) That didn't quite happen, either. Business people are still traveling in record numbers, according to the latest research.

There is no substitute for meeting face-to-face to enhance communications and to get things done. Just imagine the number of trips taken each day by government officials and their committees, not to mention business-related as well as personal travel. When it comes to important decisions, talking to each other on television just doesn't cut it. There is much value that can be garnered from traveling: to educate, inspire, discover new markets and products, meet customers and friends — the list goes on, ad infinitum. When it comes to getting the results we desire, travel is a part of the process, and a key catalyst. Sadly, businesses often think in terms of the chore rather than the opportunity: what it will cost rather than what it might bring.

In the race to create a more globally efficient and convenient world, it seems that we have been conditioned to believe that technology, together with the conveniences it affords, can somehow change our behavior and need for socializing with equal force. Anecdotal evidence would suggest otherwise. I suspect few would want to forego socializing, or even sacrifice their lifestyles, in exchange for business cost efficiency. Many do, of course, and success in business is important. To a large extent, success in life and work depends on what we are prepared to sacrifice to achieve our professional and other personal ambitions, goals and desires. Most people are unaware of the sacrifices they make. One, however, needs to be aware of what is being sacrificed in the first place, and be cognizant of the potential implications in as much as this is possible. A better quality of life is also one that is felt is real, rather than something drummed up in cyberspace.

I'm really happy that movie theaters are still around and that traveling is more popular then ever. I hope it stays that way. I, for one, have no intention of sacrificing either. In fact, it might be time to go to a movie at our old neighborhood theater near Ivy Street – yes, it's still around. Despite the doomsayers.

Are you not ashamed of heaping up

the greatest amount of

money and honor and reputation,

and caring so little about

wisdom and truth and

the greatest improvement of the soul?

—SOCRATES

LUXURY IS BEING YOURSELF

PART 1: MATERIAL LUXURY

If beauty is in the eye of the beholder, then luxury is equally so. Luxury means different things for different people, and there are just as many definitions of luxury as there are people.

The idea of luxury is more an attitude than a condition of wealth. The pursuit of luxury is done for gratification, utter comfort and a multitude of other complex personal reasons. Some people pursue riches to live in material luxury in order to differentiate themselves from the crowd, while others prefer an uncomplicated simpler life in a largely imagined world without egos. Or as Pablo Picasso once put it, 'to live a life as a poor man with lots of money'.

In the past, luxury was a term that was less complex to explain. Experts in the field will tell you that luxury is not a product, per se, but a state of mind. I agree. With the advent of better paying jobs after the Second World War, new opportunities opened up and a new environment of materialism emerged.

Opulence gained in popularity as the demand for manufactured goods escalated. As the baby boomers matured, they demanded exclusive, rare and eclectic products and services. They had the means to pay more for trendy design, fine craftsmanship and high quality, and by extension, the associated status and image.

The advent of globalization in recent times has profoundly influenced lifestyles, especially preferences for exclusivity. For some, the material luxury of an expensive watch is a sought after ambition, whilst for others, the spiritual luxury of extra time in solitude is more precious. Unlike in the past, when materialism reigned supreme, spiritualism and minimalism have impacted the psyche of the consumer as well as the need to preserve and conserve traditions and natural resources. Global luxury in the context of commercial products and services is big business, and the industry is poised to continue growing.

The same scenario seems to be playing out in China as economic progress continues to escalate. The turning point for China was the economic reforms unleashed in 1978. These reforms were the catalyst for rising incomes and led the way in raising living standards and economic prosperity over the past three decades. Growth rates, at near double-digit levels, are expected to continue into the foreseeable future.

According to Chinese government reports, times have indeed changed, and demand for luxuries are growing at a furious pace. This same phenomenon is generally true in the developed world, and in segments of the developing world.

Aside from the psychological reasons of status and prestige associated with luxury products, material luxuries come at a premium price because they are finely crafted by masters for the few who understand and appreciate fine workmanship, aesthetic beauty and exclusivity. Simply put, exceptional quality is worth more.

The notion "you get what you pay for" is well founded. Style, elegant craftsmanship and intricate designs, sometimes rare, are passed on from generation to generation in fine detail as quality products and services for a premium price. I am reminded, here, of a famous story about an American woman in Paris who asked Pablo Picasso to sketch a portrait of her. When Picasso quoted his price she asked, "why so expensive? It only took you a few minutes". "No, my dear," Picasso exclaimed, "It took me a lifetime". How does one determine price for Picasso's time or talent, or Giorgio Armani's for that matter?

Intangible attributes such as history, longevity, cachet, prestige, skill, talent, craftsmanship, vision, style, and the like are some of the hidden elements in the price. But a distinction needs to be made. The brand is not the same as the product. A product is tangible, possessing visible elements. A brand is intangible, possessing spiritual traits. For example: as fashion changes, so do the products offered by a certain brand – but the brand name does not. Price is the combination of both the product and brand. Some studies have shown that up to 40 percent of the price of a typical luxury product is compensation for its intangible worth — brand equity.

An expensive sports car might be a luxury to someone because of its craftsmanship, engineering and styling, and because it also satisfies the purchaser's egotistical needs for status and prestige. On the other hand, a simple motor scooter is just as luxurious for someone who does not have to ride the bus or a bicycle to work every day and because it also satisfies the purchaser's quest for mobility and freedom as well as prestige. What is valued, therefore, as luxury is unique, relative and situational, regardless of one's status in life. Good manners and a civilized demeanor, for instance, are also a form of luxury, especially for those who possess such qualities, and these attributes come at no cost.

During a recent symposium that I attended in Shanghai, Dr. Lu Xiong Weng, professor and deputy dean of the School of Management at Fudan University, suggested that there are four categories of people:

1. Those who have no money and no time

2. Those who have no money and have time

3. Those who have money and no time

4. Those who have money and have time

I find these distinctions or perspectives interesting and helpful in better understanding China's economic dynamism. In the simplest sense, we can surmise that economic prosperity, as it relates to luxury products and services, is a function of time and money and that, generally speaking, the people in category 4 above are the most likely to buy luxury products or services.

The race to keep up with the Joneses is an exercise in futility — and a never-ending one, at that. In the overall scheme of things, it is a waste of time and money. Luxuries ought to be noble pursuits and expressions of man's creative genius and zest for living life in beautiful and inspirational surroundings. These are manifest in many tangible and intangible ways. However, one must temper ambitions, desires and egos and keep them in balance or harmony, lest they run amok. As the old adage goes, everything in moderation and in proper perspective.

You may know all the right words,

quote the scriptures,

be brilliant in your discussions

and yet remain a bag of bones.

Or you may be inconspicuous and humble,

an insignificant person altogether,

yet glowing with loving kindness

and deep wisdom.

— NISARGADATTA, INDIAN TEACHER

LUXURY IS BEING YOURSELF

PART II: SPIRITUAL LUXURY

Status and prestige often come at a high price in a materialistic world. The idea of wanting to be (like) someone else is a preoccupation for some people; an obsession for others. An item such as an US$100,000 wristwatch is not to tell the time better, but to show the world you can afford it or, perhaps, to fulfill a yearning to be somebody else (a famous actor or a celebrity, for example). For some people, prestige comes with being associated with a certain place — say a US$500 hotel room, which then ceases to be simply a place to sleep and shower in an exotic city. Instead, it becomes a physical manifestation of one's status and power. Service par excellence, in luxurious surroundings, in exchange for premium, sometimes exorbitant, rates.

The idea of luxury manifests itself in tangible (real) and intangible (abstract) forms or a combination of both. Generally speaking, tangibles are physical products or goods, recognized and identified by our senses.

Intangibles, on the other hand, are harder to define. Since the idea of luxury exists in the mind and in the imagination, intangibles cannot be easily identified or explained. For example, they can be emotions evoked, satisfaction felt, feelings expressed or value and service appreciated. By their very natures, these conditions or states of being are forms of spiritual luxury.

As suggested in Luxury: Part One, luxury is unique for each person and does not necessarily mean extravagance or ostentation. Such a stereotype is what gives luxury a bad name. We are not interested in shallow interpretations of the new rich. Luxury is about quality not quantity, not about how many expensive things one has, which begets the question, how much is enough? The answer to this question will, of course, be personal, unique, relative and situational. Aside from the obvious material luxuries, there are spiritual forms of luxury, such as good manners and a civilized demeanor. Such qualities and attributes do not come at a cost or for a price.

There are limits to how much material riches and the relentless pursuit of an affluent lifestyle for its own sake motivates people to attain true happiness and to reach their true potential in today's unpredictable and predominantly materialistic world.

There comes a point in one's life, when after having accumulated a certain amount of wealth and experience, the pursuit of mainly tangibles is no longer the reason for being. Material things, once thought of as essential to happiness and motivation, lose their luster. Instead, other more emotionally rewarding and spiritually uplifting pursuits become more important. The ability to unconditionally choose, without external influences, while pursuing intrinsic satisfaction, is a rare luxury.

For instance, take an accomplished and wealthy individual's noble transition from entrepreneur and innovator to altruist and philanthropist. Bill Gates, and many other celebrities from all walks of life who, after having; "done it all and had it all" as the popular saying goes, felt a need to "give it back to society".

Such initiatives, on the part of "successful" (and not-so-successful) people are good examples of the benevolent use of wealth that ostensibly provide givers, at the very least, with a sense of accomplishment and the luxury of spiritual and emotional gratification. We often hear about successful people confessing that they cannot explain the exact reasons for their success or good fortune. Donald Trump perhaps sums it up best of all: everything in life, he says, is luck. This may be so; however, I have a problem with using words like "always" and "everything". Let's just say that luck is in every equation.

According to recent studies, there are basically three "real luxuries" left to pursue in today's predominantly materialistic, dynamic, highly competitive and stressful world. They are time, space, and rarity:

- Time   For ourselves and what we love to do

- Space   For privacy, reflection and peace of mind

- Rarity   What I desire that is limited and exclusive

There should be no good or bad connotation to "luxury". Luxury is culture. It is about being cultured, as well as being yourself. Sadly, not all are educated, nor brought up to have an appreciation for all things cultured and beautiful. We are not taught to understand what is good and bad taste. Such a refinement should become part of each individual's make-up, much like personality. You either have it, or you don't. Cecil B. DeMille, the famous movie mogul, used to classify people as either those who had style and refinement, or those who did not. To be oneself, and live a life that pleases you without conditions is luxury — an attitude, a state of mind if you like, shaped by perceptions. Either way, perceptions or attitude are free.

A luxury for me is travel, which is one of my favorite pastimes. Generally, the experience of travel is a much sought after product, which incidentally, has both tangible (experiential) and intangible (spiritual) elements. Travel can induce relaxation and rejuvenation, which are luxuries in their own right.

How to make the best use of time and money is each individual's prerogative. It is more an issue of what is appropriate, under the circumstances than what's right or wrong. Pursuing luxuries and comforts is an intricate and essential part of the human condition, and does not have to be a zero-sum game. There are no winners or losers. Happiness and contentedness is somewhere in the balance — somewhere between too much, too expensive and too little, too inexpensive, and largely depends on one's financial means and dreams.

Finally, we want more than just appearances, beauty and style. We also want substance and intrinsic value. Generally speaking, pursuing a life of luxurious living in all its forms and manifestations comes at a price. Everyone, regardless of social strata, is a player to some degree in this wonderful game. We are constantly trading off one thing for another. As the old saying goes, nothing in life is for free. You either pay, or you sacrifice. For me, luxury means many things. Some can be had for a premium price while others cannot. In the final analysis, and at this point in my life, foremost amongst these are other people doing things for me that I don't like to do myself — and someday owning a Porsche.

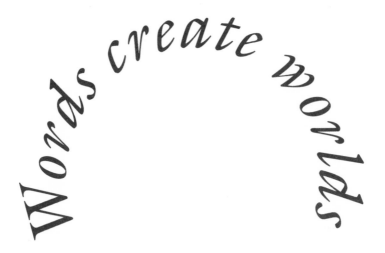

Words create worlds

—LUDWIG WITTGENSTEIN
AUSTRIAN PHILOSOPHER

THE SCIENCE OF SEMANTICS

Boutique hotels have made an indelible mark on the global hotel scene, as witnessed by their proliferation and publicity. Compared to their mainstream counterparts, they are more "exclusive," and therefore pricier. Chief amongst the reasons for their popularity is their striking architecture, small size and impressive minimalist designs, highly personalized service, eclectic amenities and innovative cuisine. Such hotels generally appeal to a more urban, affluent, younger and more educated generation of users. They are ideal places for hedonists — people who pursue pleasure for the sake of pleasure — and, of course, the chosen few who can afford them.

On the one hand, the battle to win the affluent hotel customer in all corners of the globe continues at a rapid clip. The explosion of boutique hotels, along with newer and more modern hotels, creates problems for many of the older or "first generation" hotels that find it tougher to compete in this new environment, because they have allowed themselves to become anachronisms. The symptoms: aging without the benefits of periodic upgrading and modernization and failing to stay abreast of change.

Hotel promotion lingo, on the other hand, is migrating from a focus on the basics of the product itself and its physical attributes. (Hopefully this will also mean the permanent retirement of the rather worn out "home away from home" tagline that is often used in generic hotel advertising to describe the hotel stay experience as well.) The new trend is more sensual in style and tone, and designed to appeal to the senses — a promise that we will 'revive, renew, relax and rejuvenate' you. No, you won't be checking into an overnight Spa – but it's close.

Avoiding what is destined to become tomorrow's clutter of like-minded promotional messages is going to be challenging enough for marketers as they attempt to differentiate their products and services. Another is sameness in hotel design. It is becoming more and more difficult to distinguish between hotels these days, because most hotels look and feel the same. This is perhaps one reason why some people tend to identify more with the brand — the name of the place — rather than the physical product itself. No surprise that the focus is once again being placed on branding.

Branding goes beyond selling, and is an effective means of differentiating products and services. It focuses more attention on the "intangible" aspects of the relationship between products or brands and targeted customers — the rather fuzzy invisible spiritual and emotional connections — and, to a lesser extent, on the "tangibles"— the more visible and physical aspects of a product or service to create a lasting bond, on their own, with customers. This is nothing new. For decades, enlightened promoters have been very much aware of the power of pushing the intangibles to win the ego. These 'engineers of perception' are busy at work creating new realities, new messages and emotionally charged advertising campaigns with rejuvenating promises and associated images of nirvana. These new campaigns, I figure, are destined to work in the new emerging hotel world of hedonism.

For hotels in particular, renewed focus on branding and the idea of revival are welcome and timely trends. For centuries, travel and tourism, by their very natures, have been catalysts for nourishing the mind and the spirit, a means for renewal and revitalization, amongst other things. By extension, hotels are part of the same fabric, the same industry. I first learned about branding watching cowboy films as a youngster. It was something they did to cows. I hope marketers don't think of me as a cow as they try to revive me. Then again, if branding (the advertising and promotion kind) didn't work, why would companies spend millions every year doing it to us?

Wanting & Waiting

Happiness is an illusion

Unless it is felt

Not a goal to be met;

Wanting and waiting

Happiness is contentedness

When it is felt

From goals already met;

Wanting not waiting

—PETER ALATSAS

OFF THE HOOK

They say the simple things in life are free. In Japan, they are also sensational. Simplicity, after all, is an expression of elegance. Take Ikebana. The simplicity and beauty of this form of Japanese flower arrangement is fascinating. For one, Ikebana represents the Japanese passion for nature, and like most art forms, this one is difficult to describe with words. In addition to representing the love of flower arrangement, this expression "seeks tranquility and perfection which lies in its asymmetrical balance, respect for the individual flower and harmony with nature as a whole". Even Samurai learned Ikebana to practice concentration.

Practicing concentration is more difficult in today's emotionally disconnected world than in the days of the samurai. I became aware of this phenomenon whilst living in gizmo crazy Japan in the late 90s. Paradoxically, many people in so-called technologically advanced countries are in many ways "disconnected in a connected world" according to behaviorists. What on earth does this mean?

With so much time spent on television, cell phones, messaging, MP3 players, games, computers and the internet, people have little or no time at all for themselves and for others — for human connectivity. They have become, in a sense, emotionally disconnected from their loved ones, and the things they really like to do in the new technologically advanced and interconnected world. This phenomenon exists in practically every technologically advanced society and the consequences, they say, are bound to have repercussions for both mental and physical health.

Escaping routines and addictions, such as the overuse of electronic devices, to maintain a proper balance is difficult in the present environment and sometimes hard to understand or explain.

I frequently attend business meetings where many of the participants are glued to their computer screens, ostensibly working on very important things whilst trying to keep an ear on the proceedings. From time to time, they will tune in, offering a contribution to make people think that they are engaged and listening. Then, it's back to the keyboard. Or they will buzz out to answer their buzzing cell phones. How many times can you go to the washroom? And when they really get bored, they engage in frantic messaging, coyly resting their cell phones on their laps under the table like amateur sleuths — as if no one really knew what was going on. On one occasion, I recall hardly seeing the face of one of the participants in a meeting.

Some people should just loosen up and stop taking themselves so seriously and "get a life". For starters, the notion of "wanting" and not "waiting" for some divine inspiration to get them, and all of us, off the hook should be inspiration enough. The right attitude is everything.

It is the chiefest point of happiness that man is willing to be what he is

—Desiderius Erasmus

THE NEVER-ENDING JOURNEY

It has been said that life is a game, and that everything is invented -- presumably in the mind. The idea takes on a new meaning in Greece. Being of Greek origin, I am forever trying to reconcile past and present. In any case, I find myself somewhere in between: nowhere. Generally speaking, this predominantly seafaring nation is a magnanimous and friendly place, made up of mostly emotionally charged and highly impulsive wanderers and dreamers who are just as quick to tears as to laughter. Paradoxically, when overcome by joy they are moved to tears; when sad, they laugh. I reckon that such a complexity mainly springs from two ideas: one, that worrying is futile, and secondly, not taking themselves too seriously.

In the famous novel, *Zorba the Greek*, by Nikos Kazantzakis, Zorba is full of dreams and a zest for life that includes misplaced optimism. This fictional character is a metaphor for the appreciation of joy and sadness that co-exists in life. His pursuit of happiness for its own sake reaches a point of madness. There are real-life examples, as well: the (rather wasteful) Greek tradition of breaking plates whilst in a state of euphoria or joy is a nicer, gentler form of madness, if there is such a thing,

Hardship and disappointment are a function of everyday life, but their effects can be minimized with travel and restoration. Travel offers a change of scenery. Anecdotal evidence suggests that a mere change of scenery is both relaxing and therapeutic, and helps restore one to a state of well being, much like the effect of a good cry. Tears, by one definition are a form of restoration; they help to return us to a happier state of being and elation. Such is the complexity of life.

Maintaining a positive mental attitude even in the worst of times is essential. The idea of "wanting" to feel good all the time is a start. A pathos to keep on going when all else fails, or when things can't get any worse: easier said than done, but not impossible. Positive words, in a way, act as catalysts or as coping mechanisms. Oftentimes, certain negative words like "loneliness" and "boredom" become self-fulfilling prophecies in that you get the behavior you expect. Imagine a world without these words. Let's take them out of our vocabulary altogether. Let us not become a manifestation of the very negative words or ideas that we think and speak.

On final reflection, perhaps it's the beauty of the place that brings out the best and worst in us. The mythical gods blessed Greece with an abundance of beauty, words and stories to inspire and invigorate the body, mind and spirit. And, of course, without a past there is no future. Perhaps this is why the relentless pursuit for meaning is an endless endeavor in such a place, as well. Nowhere is this more prevalent, at least in my view, than in Greece. You will invariably enjoy the trip. The journey, however, never ends.

Himself

Self-Made Man
Behind the Persona

Sole vessel:
...of illusion in a sea of perceptions
...of sanity in a sea of stupidity
...of serenity in a sea of pretense
...of tranquility in a sea of invention

Self-Made Man
That Worships his Creator

—PETER ALATSAS

IDIOT SABBATICAL

Here's a thought: How about paying more attention to stupidity, in all its manifestations?

Researchers at the Lindbergh University Medical Center in Sweden claim that stress can be fatal — and working with stupid people is one of the deadliest forms of stress, contributing even to heart attacks.

A recent study by Dr. Dagmar Anderson revealed that 62 percent of the 500 heart attack patients her team studied had relatively few of the risk factors known to cause heart attacks. But some of the patients claimed that they suffered heart attacks after confrontations with idiots, and their stupidity. One woman had to be rushed to hospital after her assistant shredded important company documents, instead of copying them. Another woman spent a week rebuilding client records because a clerk put them in the "recycle bin" of her computer and then emptied it (thinking the records would be recycled and used again). Imagine the countless stories, told and untold, about stupidity inside and outside of the workplace.

The wise doctor concludes, 'Most people have very poor coping skills when it comes to stupidity. They feel that there is nothing they can do about it, so they internalize their frustration until they finally explode". After having made my own contributions to the natural science of stupidity for the better part of half a century, one might be advised to eat well, exercise regularly, stop smoking and stay clear of idiots as much as possible.

Traveling is one possible respite. Synthesizing the journey and the destination can add to the enjoyment. Going someplace is one thing, getting there is another.

Both experiences should not be viewed in isolation. All it takes is a change of attitude. Many people simply dread the idea of traveling in a post 9-11 world. No need to fear, just factor in the new reality. This will also boost your level of tolerance necessary for travel in the first place.

A change of scenery, even for a short period of time, can be therapeutic if for no other reason than the peace of mind that can come from escaping routine (including the idiots, of course). The Japanese have made the "short and frequent" vacation trips an art form, albeit for mostly economic and cultural reasons. This is a trend that is fast replacing the "once in a lifetime trip", and who knows – its popularity may well grow, for health reasons.

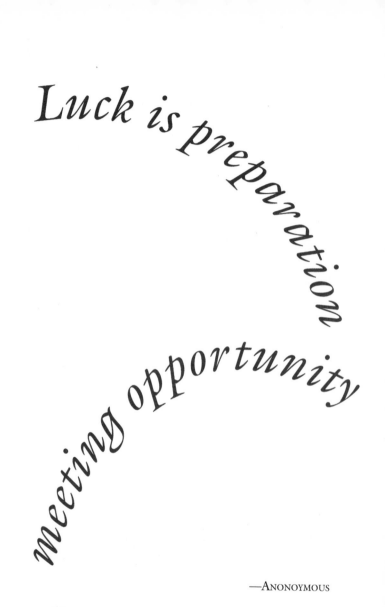

Luck is preparation meeting opportunity

—ANONOYMOUS

Aspirations and Inspirations
(or is it the other way around?)

C harles Kemmons Wilson was the founder of Holiday Inn Hotels. He was born an only child in Arkansas. His father died when he was 9 months old and the family moved to Memphis, where his mother, Doll, got a job as a dental assistant.

Doll Wilson lost her job during the Great Depression, and the young Charles had to leave high school to work. He borrowed $50 from a friend, bought himself a popcorn machine and placed it in the lobby of a movie theater. This was the beginning of what would be a series of successful entrepreneurial ventures. A few years later, he managed to save $1,700 from this small business venture and bought a house for himself and his mother. He then mortgaged the house to invest in a Wurlitzer jukebox franchise.

While vacationing in Washington, D.C., he became annoyed by the high prices families had to pay to stay in hotels, and came up with the idea of creating a hotel chain where children could stay for free. He built the first four Holiday Inns in Memphis. The rest is history.

According to early accounts, Wilson designed the famous Holiday Inn sign using his earlier experience selling popcorn at movie theaters. (The name Holiday Inn was taken from a Bing Crosby film.) "I knew the value of a marquee. I said I wanted a sign at least 50 feet tall and to have a marquee on it," Wilson said in 1989.

Wilson was characterized as down-to-earth and very hard-working. Like many modern-day corporate celebrities, he too had a list of 20 tips for success. One of the more famous: "Only work half a day. It doesn't matter which half – the first 12 hours or the second 12 hours." (And, I suppose, as the old saying goes, the harder he worked, the luckier he got.) He also had the uncanny ability to persuade people to lend him money – a hard-to-teach, but extremely valuable skill!

Luck is in every equation for success. There are, of course, many other factors as well, such as daring, character, good timing and intellect. Edward De Bono, whose claims can console those who aspire to equal greatness, said, 'You don't have to be intelligent to be a good thinker."

Like most travelers, I am inspired by the things I notice when I travel. Oftentimes, what catapults people to greatness is a simple idea, and behind every idea there is some sort of inspiration. Who knows: aspiration for greatness, and the inspiration for the next big idea just might come up during your next vacation. It worked for Wilson.

An intelligent decision
is based on what you know

A wise decision
is based on what you do
with what you know

—ALAIN DE BOTTON

InSPAration

Enticed by a particularly alluring marketing brochure, I recently visited a well-known spa. Despite the fact that spas are perceived to be a female extravagance, I wasn't disappointed. Let's face it, when it comes to pampering and self-indulgence, men have a lot to learn from women. I came to the party rather late, so to speak. Spa treatments just weren't a part of my usual routine, but after submitting to what turned out to be an orgy of the senses, they just might become one.

Spas have been around for centuries, and like bottled water, they can be found practically everywhere these days, thanks to the savvy promoters and marketers that are fueling their proliferation. Such places of hedonism are all the rage, and hotels in particular are eager to add them to their stable of product offerings. Some purveyors, encouraged by their newfound promise, are literally falling over each other in an effort to cash into what is essentially an ancient idea repackaged as a new trend.

After surrendering myself to the capable hands (and control) of my Thai therapist, I was on my way, and as the brochure promised, I entered into a "sanctuary of the senses". I entered into a world of deep reflection as well as enjoyment, thanks to the ambience and the very experience itself: the body treatments, soothing music, scents, oils, and the like. At times, I would fall into various stages of sleep, only to be jolted back to reality by the gentle therapist, who was eager to beam me to the next phase of treatment for what was to be a four-hour journey into bliss.

In the words of the brochure, I was to be "induced with therapeutic rejuvenation". And I was. I felt this sense of overwhelming emancipation from bodily stress and strain and often drifted, as a consequence, into deep thought.

Strangely enough, my thoughts were philosophical in nature — possibly because I had just finished reading a splendid book by one of my favorite writers: Alain de Botton's *The Consolation of Philosophy*. On reflection, my decision to go through with this idea in the first place was a wise, rather than an intelligent one. An intelligent decision, according to de Botton, is based on what you know. A wise decision, on the other hand, is based on what you do with what you know.

Paradoxically, the sometimes complex stuff of philosophy (although made easy to understand in this book) did not deter me from relaxing and enjoying myself. One possible explanation is the surrendering of the senses to the delights of pampering. Who doesn't like to be pampered? While being under, I reached the following (if I may say) rather profound and wise assessment: the best time to visit a spa is after you have finished a good book, rather than after an argument, let's say, with a boss or spouse.

Winning isn't everything

It's the only thing

—Vince Lombardi

THE WORLD IN A CUP

O n the day of the final between France and Italy (circa 2006), soccer lovers worldwide were wrapped up in activities surrounding the World Cup. After all, there are more countries represented by FIFA, the world body that governs soccer, than in the United Nations. I, too, was wrapped up comfortably in my hotel bed in Osaka when the wake-up call came at 2.30 am. "Time to go," said the surprisingly strong and wide-awake voice at the other end. My co-worker in the next room had kept his promise to wake me up so that we could watch the final game on a big screen at a neighborhood bar just a few blocks from our hotel.

Walking the short distance in the wee hours of the morning was rather peaceful and serene, in sharp contrast to the scene at the bar. There, the (mostly male) audience chatted impatiently, awaiting the start of the game, yet managed to remain civilized and well composed, in that inimitable Japanese way. Refreshments had been lined up in front of patrons to avoid interruptions during the game. To my surprise, most were wearing Italian kits. Amazing, I thought to myself, in Japan, of all places, where almost everything French is considered fashionable (even when it's not). Perhaps the Italian edge was that their players were better looking? Certainly, as far as which was the better team, the odds were even.

These days, sports are oftentimes used as a metaphor for effective leadership in the cliché-drenched world of business. Take the idea of teamwork: "team players" are highly sought after in both sports and business – yet paradoxically, teamwork is the result of individual effort. Skill and "fit" into a group depends, in large part, on the individual. , Whether the aim is scoring goals or making profits, all team members have to perform at their personal best. Teamwork, or harmony in execution, is not a goal, but an outcome – the result of each individual team member's efforts. Teamwork is realized when many activities come together in the form of results. Staying in the game and in the competition is everything.

In the end, results are what matter most. Playing a good game and not winning it, or running a good business that is marginally profitable, might be entertaining enough, but is no real fun in the overall scheme of things. "Winning isn't everything," say the runners-up — but it's still a lot better to win than to lose. Money isn't everything either, but especially for those who lack it, it's better to have it, than not. That analogy applies to quite a few of life's resources – like, say, hair. For my near-balding friends, who look wistfully upon my full head of hair, and remind me to get a haircut, hair is everything.

Speaking of heads, and bald ones at that, did Zinedine's Zidan's head-butting the chest of Marco Materazzi really deserve all that fuss? We may never learn what was said, as there was no witness to corroborate either side. Did the lip readers get it right? Who cares? It's all part of the beautiful game, albeit made temporarily ugly for a few minutes by anger – temporary insanity. Zinedine got sent off, as he should have, and will probably be penalized for two or three future games, as he should. Justice was served.

The game of soccer is affectionately known as the beautiful game. That it is, especially when played with grace and professionalism. It's all about enjoyment, entertainment, skill, style and finishes, results … scoring magnificent goals and, as in business, making lots of money. The more, the better.

FOOD
FOR
THOUGHT

from the Great Thinkers and Philosophers

ON THE PAST * PRESENT * FUTURE

"Even God cannot change the past."

—AGATHON

"Study the past if you would divine the future."

—CONFUCIUS

"The distinction between past, present and future is only a stubbornly persistent illusion."

—EINSTEIN

ON CHARACTER AND PERSONALITY

"Most men are within a fingers' breadth of being mad."

—DIOGENES

"It is easy to perform a good action, but not easy to acquire a settled habit of performing such actions."

—ARISTOTLE

"Character is higher than intellect."

—RALPH WALDO EMERSON

*"A good style must, first of all, be clear.
It must.... be appropriate."*

—ARISTOTLE

*"Kindness in words creates confidence.
Kindness in thinking creates profoundness.
Kindness in giving creates love."*

—LAO TZU

*"A man never discloses his own character so clearly
as when he describes another's."*

—J.P.RICHTER

*"Great minds discuss IDEAS
Average minds discuss EVENTS
Small minds discuss PEOPLE."*

—HUGH C. CAMERON

*"You never get a second chance to make a good first
impression."*

—PROVERB

"Courage is not the lack of fear. It is acting in spite of it."

—PROVERB

"He acts before he speaks, and afterwards speaks according to his actions."

—CONFUCIUS

"Man will do many things to get himself loved; he will do all things to get himself envied."

—MARK TWAIN

ON FATE, DESTINY & LUCK

"One must not tie a ship to a single anchor or life to a single hope."

—EPICTETUS

"He who submits to fate without complaint is wise."

—EURIPIDES

"Everywhere man blames nature and fate, yet his fate is mostly but the echo of his character and passions, his mistakes and weaknesses."

—DEMOCRITUS

"As God disposes, man laughs or weeps."

—SOPHOCLES

"Everything in life is luck."

—DONALD TRUMP

"Destiny is something that is achieved, not given."

—GREEK PROVERB

ON HAPPINESS

"Happiness is self-contentedness."

—ARISTOTLE

"Happiness resides not in possessions and not in gold, the feeling of happiness dwells in the soul."

—DEMOCRITUS

*"It is not good for all you wish to be fulfilled:
through sickness you recognize the value of health,
through evil the value of good,
through hunger satisfaction,
through exertion the value of rest."*

—HERACLITUS

*"If you have a wounded heart, touch it as little as
you would an injured eye. There are only two
remedies for the injured soul: Hope and Patience."*

—PYTHAGORAS

*"A pleasant and happy life does not come from
external things. Man draws from within himself,
as from a spring, pleasure and joy."*

—PLUTARCH

"Happiness is the absence of the striving for happiness."

—CHUANG-TZU

*"It is the chiefest point of happiness that man is
willing to be what he is."*

—DESIDERIUS ERASMUS

"May the happiest days of your past be the saddest days of your future."

—ANONYMOUS

ON IDEAS

❧

"Credit goes to the person who convinces the world, not to the one to whom the idea first occurs."

—SIR WILLIAM OSTER

"Men are not worried by things, but by their ideas about things."

—EPICTETUS

"When we meet with difficulties, become anxious or troubled, let us not blame others, but rather ourselves — that is, our ideas about things."

—EPICTETUS

"Without knowing the force of words, it is impossible to know men."

—CONFUCIUS

"If one is able to acquire new knowledge by reviewing old knowledge, he is qualified to be a tutor."

—CONFUCIUS

"Keep on the lookout for novel ideas that others have used successfully. Your idea has to be original only in its adaptation to the problem you are working on."

—THOMAS ALVA EDISON

"Words create Worlds."

—LUDWIG WITTGENSTEIN

"The principlal mark of genius is not perfection, but or+grnality."

—PLATO

"They may forget what you said, but they will never forget how you made them feel."

—MAYA ANGELOU

ON HUMAN BEHAVIOR

*"Human behavior flows from three main sources:
Desire, Emotion, and Knowledge."*

—PLATO

*"If man is moderate and contented, then even age is
no burden. If he is not, then even youth is full of cares.*

—PLATO

"Man: a being in search of meaning."

—PLATO

"Man is a political animal."

—ARISTOTLE

*"Once made equal to man, woman becomes his
superior."*

—SOCRATES

*"One who rises, rises of himself
One who falls, falls from himself."*

—NI BITTSU

*"What the gentleman seeks, he seeks within himself;
what the small man seeks, he seeks in others."*

—CONFUCIUS

*"I hear and I forget
I see and I remember
I do and I understand."*

—CHINESE PROVERB

*"Boys do not learn to honor their fathers.
They are taught by their mothers."*

—CHINESE PROVERB

ON PHILOSOPHY

*"Wonder is the feeling of a philosopher, and
philosophy begins in wonder."*

—SOCRATES (470-399)

"My belief is to have no wants is Divine."

—SOCRATES

"There is a desire deep within the soul which drives man from the seen to the unseen, to philosophy and the divine."

—KAHLIL GIBRAN

"There is no answer, there never was an answer, there never will be an answer. That's the answer."

—GERTRUDE STEIN

ON WISDOM

"The beginning of wisdom is the definition of terms."

—SOCRATES

" The only good is knowledge and the only evil is ignorance."

—SOCRATES

"We can be knowledgeable with other men's knowledge, but we cannot be wise with other men's wisdom."

—MICHEL DE MONTAGNE

"All our knowledge has its origins in our perceptions."

—LEONARDO DA VINCI

"By three methods we may learn wisdom:
First, by reflection, which is noblest;
Second, by imitation which is easiest;
and third by experience, which is the bitterest."

—CONFUCIUS

"You may know all the right words,
quote the scriptures, be brilliant in your
discussions and yet remain a bag of bones.

Or you may be inconspicuous and humble,
an insignificant person altogether, yet glowing
with loving kindness and deep wisdom."

—NISARGADATTA, INDIAN TEACHER

"Wisdom consists of the anticipation of consequences."

—NORMAN COUSINS

" I have never met a man so ignorant that I
couldn't learn something from him."

—GALILEO GALILEI

ON WEALTH

"If a rich man is proud of his wealth, he should not be praised until it is known how he employs it."

—SOCRATES

"Are you not ashamed of heaping up the greatest amount of money and honor and reputation, and caring so little about wisdom and truth and the greatest improvement of the soul?"

—SOCRATES

"Remember, no human condition is ever permanent, then you will not be overjoyed in good fortune, nor too sorrowful in misfortune."

—SOCRATES

ON ATTITUDE

"Behave towards everyone as if receiving a great guest."

—CONFUCIUS

"The superior man bends his attention to what is radical.
That being established, all practical courses naturally grow up."

—CONFUCIUS

"The superior man thinks always of virtue; the common man thinks of comfort."

—CONFUCIUS

"Be friendly and attentive to the needs of others for men cannot reach fulfillment alone; help improve society, for men must depend on it for their attainment."

—CONFUCIUS

"The superior man makes demands on himself. The inferior man makes demands on others."

—CONFUCIUS

"Kindness is the source of all values."

—CONFUCIUS

"To be wronged is nothing unless you continue to remember it."

—CONFUCIUS

"*The superior man understands what is right. The inferior man understands what will sell.*"

—Confucius

'*Don't worry about being misunderstood, but about understanding others.*'

—Confucius

"*Nothing is interesting if you are not interested.*"

—Helen MacIness

"*The greatest discovery of his time was that human beings could alter their lives by altering their attitudes of mind.*"

—William James

"*The great always introduce us to facts. Small men introduce us always to themselves.*"

—Proverb

"*Logic takes you from point A to B. Imagination takes you everywhere.*"

—Einstein

"*Practice being content and you will become carefree.*"

—Proverb

"*Only those who respect themselves have the courage to humble themselves even more.*"

—PROVERB

"*Health is the greatest gift, contentment the greatest wealth, faithfulness the best relationship.*"

—BUDDHA

ON EXPERIENCE & WORK

"*Everything has been thought of before, but the problem is to think of it again.*"

—JOHANN W. VON GOETHE

"*An ounce of image is worth a pound of performance.*"

—LAURENCE J. PETER

"*Yesterday's clarity is today's stupidity.*"

—IKKYU-ZEN MONK

"An error does not have to become a mistake unless you correct it."

—JOHN F. KENNEDY

"The world is big enough for everyone's needs, but not enough for everyone's greed."

—ANWAR IBRAHIM

"Experience is not what happens to a man — it is what a man does with what happens to him."

—ALDOUS HUXLEY

"Take away the cause, and the effect ceases."

—MANUEL DE CERVANTES

"The gem cannot be polished without friction, nor man perfected without trial."

—PROVERB

"Our aspirations are our possibilities."

—ROBERT BROWNING

"The gentleman helps others to realize what is good in them. He does not help them realize what is bad in them. The small man does the opposite."

—CONFUCIUS

"Choose a job you love, and you will never have to work a day in your life."

—CONFUCIUS

"Wishing to be established oneself, one helps others become established. Wishing to be successful oneself, one helps others be successful."

—CONFUCIUS

If we take people as we find them, we may make them worse,
But if we treat them as though they are what they should be, we help them to become what they are capable of becoming."

—JOHANN W. VON GOETHE

"Before you can become somebody, you have to be that somebody."

——JOHANN W. VON GOETHE

"Leadership is influence."

——JOHN C. MAXWELL

ON MONEY

"The thing that I should wish to obtain from money would be leisure with security."

—BERTRAND RUSSELL

"It is not the employer who pays the wages — he only handles the money. It is the product that pays the wages."

—HENRY FORD

"I'd like to live like a poor man with lots of money."

—PABLO PICASSO

"Money often costs too much."

—RALPH WALDO EMERSON

"As a general rule, nobody has money who ought to have it."

—BENJAMIN DISRAELI

"When it comes to money, everybody is of the same religion."

—VOLTAIRE

"When you see what some girls marry, you realize how they must hate to work for a living."

—HELEN ROWLAND

"Better to be an old mans' darling than a young man's slave."

—PROVERB

"A rich man's joke is always funny."

—PROVERB

ON CULTURE

"Home is not where you live but where they understand you."

—CHRISTIAN MORGENSTERN

Men's natures are alike — it is their habits that carry them far apart.

—PROVERB

"By nature, all men are pretty much alike. It is by custom and habit that they are set apart."

—CONFUCIUS

ON LIFE

"Life can only be understood backwards, but must be lived forwards."

—SOREN KIERKEGARD

"Life is not a problem to be solved, but a reality to be experienced."

—SOREN KIERKEGARD

"One's only real life is the life one never leads."

—OSCAR WILDE

"The less of routine, the more of life."

—A. B. ALCOTT

"The good life starts only when you stop wanting a better one."

—BERTRAND RUSSELL

"As I grow to understand life less and less, I learn to live it more and more."

—JULES RENARD

"Forget not that the earth delights to feel your bare feet and the winds long to play with your hair."

—KAHLIL GIBRAN

"The man who has no inner life is the salve of his surroundings."

—HENRI-FREDERIC AMIEL

"The tragedy of life is what dies inside a man while he lives."

—ALBERT SCHWEITZER

'Forty is the old age of youth; fifty the youth of old age.'

—VICTOR HUGO

"No man is a failure who is enjoying life."

—WILLIAM FEATHER

"We do not have a claim on our life, but only the right to use it."

—PROVERB

"A person is only a person through other people."

—AFRICAN PROVERB

ON TIME

"The time you enjoy wasting is not wasted time."

—BERTRAND RUSSELL

"Time, like death, is absent yet present."

—PROVERB

"If you can make good use of time, you can surely go where you want to go."

—PROVERB

ON CHANGE

"Half of what we are teaching today will be obsolete tomorrow. Only we do not know which half."

—PROVERB

"Men don't change. The only thing new in the world is the history you don't know."

—HARRY S. TRUMAN

"The thinking that got us here is incapable of getting us out of here."

—EINSTEIN

"It is not the strongest of the species that survives, nor the most intelligent that survives. It is the one that is most adaptable to change."

—CHARLES DARWIN

ON LUCK

"Luck is preparation meeting opportunity."

—ANONYMOUS

ON TRAVEL & LEISURE

"To travel hopefully is better than to arrive."

—Sir James Jeans

"Wheresoever you go, go with all your heart."

—Confucius

"The best intelligence is what we do with our leisure."

—Ernest Benn

"Liberty is being free from the things we don't like in order to be slaves to the things we do like."

—Ernest Benn

"Business travelers can be 'sold' but not 'bought'.

—Proverb

"Tranquility comes when the mind concentrates."

—Proverb

ON CHILDREN

"Children begin by loving their parents. After a time, they judge them. Rarely, if ever, do they forgive them."

—OSCAR WILDE

"Nothing makes a child happier than a happy parent."

—GREEK PROVERB

"When I was a boy of 14, my father was so ignorant I could hardly stand to have the old man around. But when I got to be 21, I was astonished at how much the old man had learned in seven years."

—MARK TWAIN

ON INTEGRITY & TRUTH

❧

*"Persecution cannot harm him who stands by truth.
Did not Socrates fall proudly a victim of body?
Was not Paul stoned for the sake of the truth? It
is our inner selves that hurt us when we disobey it,
and it kills us when we betray it."*

—KAHLIL GIBRAN

*"When you are sorrowful, look again in your heart,
and you shall see that in truth you are weeping for
that which has been your delight."*

—KAHLIL GIBRAN

*"A lie can travel half way around the world while
the truth is putting on its shoes."*

—MARK TWAIN

*"A lie becomes truth — only if the person wants to
believe it."*

—PROVERB

ON POETRY

"Inside every man there is a poet who died young."

—STEFAN KANFER

"No poems can live long or please that are written by water drinkers."

—HORACE

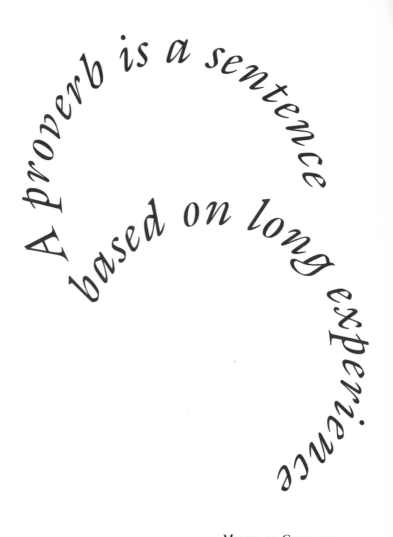

A proverb is a sentence based on long experience

—Miguel de Cervantes

THE CRACKED POT

In ancient China, women would carry pots down to the village stream to get fresh water for the day's cooking and bathing. The pots were hung on the end of a pole, one on each end, and carried across the neck. There was once a woman whose pot cracked – not enough to break, but enough to leak. At the end of the long walk from the stream to the house, the cracked pot always arrived only half full, while the perfect pot delivered all its water intact.

This went on for two years, and every day, the woman brought home only one and a half pots of water. Naturally, the perfect pot was proud of itself. But the poor cracked pot was ashamed, and miserable that it could only do half its job.

Finally, after two years of failure, the cracked pot could stand it no more. As the woman was scooping water from the stream, it spoke. "I am so ashamed," it said. "This crack in my side means that water leaks all the way back to your house." To its surprise, the woman smiled. "Yes, but did you notice that there are flowers on your side of the path, but not on the other pot's side?

"That's because I have always known about your flaw, so I planted flower seeds on your side of the path. Every day while we walk back, you water them. For two years, I have been able to pick these beautiful flowers to decorate the house. If you weren't just the way your are, I wouldn't have this beauty in the house."

Each of us has our own unique flaw. But it is the cracks and flaws that we each have that make our lives together so very interesting and rewarding. You've just got to take each person for what they are, and look for the good in them. Even a broken clock, as an old Greek saying goes, gets the time right twice a day.

Experience is a hard teacher because she gives the tests first and the lessons later

—Vernon Law

LIFE'S WISDOM

Valuable lessons, learned over the years

✸ LIFE WITH OTHERS

Trust is at the heart of every relationship.

Everything happens for a reason. Make the most of every situation.

What people think happens is more important than what happens. Perception is reality most of the time.

Nothing stays "fixed" for too long.

Home is not where you live, but where you are loved.

People don't care how much you know until they know how much you care.

✸ YOUR LIFE

You are the most powerful when you are yourself.

You are the words you speak.

You are ultimately defined by your actions.

To reach true potential, compare yourself with yourself
— not with others.

Harbor positive thoughts and act on them
— attitude is everything.

Judge yourself by what you can do, not what you can't do.

Happiness is a place between too little and too much.

Destiny is what happens when you are indecisive,
or fail to take charge.

Don't live in a world other people create.

Don't live in the past, but learn from the past.

❊ WORKING LIFE

Business is not about being fair. It's about being effective
in your relationships with people.

Power is about perceived dependence.

You get the behavior you reward.
The way to get failure is to expect it.
People like to learn, but don't like to be taught.

Un-learning is more difficult than learning.

Everything is difficult before it becomes easy.

Listen to understand not to respond.

There are no difficult tasks, just unfamiliar ones.

Don't raise prices without raising value.

Quality is remembered long after price is forgotten.

There is no safety in playing it safe. Take charge.

When looking to change jobs, never throw away
dirty water before you have clean. The worst time
to find a job is when you need one.

If they want you, they will find you.

POSTSCRIPT

Before you set off on your own endless journey, remember that the key to exploring the world is to do it with style and wonder — in your own way and on your own terms — with an open and inquisitive mind and, of course, the right attitude. Discover with the spirit of an adventurer and the imagination of a dreamer who is always looking, as the Chinese saying goes, to find a "rounder moon" in foreign lands (even when you are stuck in the transient lounge that is organized life.) And, as Confucius observed many hundreds of years ago, *wheresoever you go, go with all your heart.*

Don't put off that journey. You can't live life to the fullest by continuously putting things off for next time. There is no "next time", only "this time". Next time is a logical fallacy, a trap we fall into — you can never step into the same river twice, as the old Chinese saying goes.

Everything new is free

The writings contained in this book are nothing more than opinions and perspectives on various aspects of travel and on life in general. It is inspired by the notion 'everything new is free' — a new attitude, a new beginning, a new idea, a new relationship. We are all the same, and all different. We all see the same things, and think of them in different ways.

It takes a (global) village

They say that it takes a village to raise a child — and it has taken a global village to make this book idea into a reality. The selected essays or short stories that make up this book first appeared in a monthly column, "Travel Plan Insights", in *Travel Plan* magazine, published in Japan for the hotel and tourism trade, and for this, I thank Mike Pokrovsky, the managing editor, and his father, George, the publisher (more on George later).

In Japan, Julien Ritter, an English teacher, was kind enough to lend his editing skills to my pieces before they were submitted to *Travel Plan*. In Shanghai, it was a chance conversation at the pastry counter with Tina Kanagaratnam of AsiaMedia that created the spark that turned these articles into a book — my thanks to her for ably weaving the disparate articles together into this volume. And my thanks to Feng Lei, AsiaMedia's talented designer, who gave this book its very special look.

Finally, my thanks to George Pokrovsky, the publisher of Travel Plan, who introduced me to the idea of writing. "Why not write a column for my magazine?" he asked over cocktails at the Tokyo Press Club. "I am not a writer, George," I replied. Not easily dissuaded, George wouldn't take 'no' for an answer. "Do it," he insisted, adding rather flatteringly, "I like the way you think." And in the end, that's what this book is: a collection of my thoughts, of my thinking. Thank you, George, for your encouragement and friendship – it has made all the difference.